# IN THE PATH OF
# HITLER'S
# THIRD REICH

# IN THE PATH OF
# HITLER'S THIRD REICH

## THE JOURNEY FROM VICTORY TO DEFEAT

## IAN WESTWELL

GRAMERCY BOOKS

NEW YORK

First published in 1998 by
PRC Publishing Ltd,
Kiln House, 210 New Kings Road, London SW6 4NZ

© 1998 by Random House Value Publishing, Inc.

This edition is published by Gramercy Books,®
a division of Random House Value Publishing, Inc.,
201 East 50th Street, New York, New York, 10022.

Gramercy Books® and design are registered trademarks of
Random House Value Publishing, Inc.

Random House
New York • Toronto • London • Sydney • Auckland
http://www.randomhouse.com/

Printed and bound in China

A CIP catalogue record for this book is available from the Library of Congress.

ISBN 0-517-16048-X

8 7 6 5 4 3 2 1

**Note about Anglicization**

It is always difficult to be precise about the anglicization of German—so many of the words
(eg: *Luftwaffe, Führer, Reich, Gestapo*) have become so common that translation is unnecessary.
In the main, therefore, the more usual forms have been used untranslated, including place
names. However, those places more usually anglicized (Nuremberg for *Nürnberg*, Hanover for
*Hannover*, Brunswick for *Braunschweig*, Munich for *München*) have been, and terms and ranks
with straightforward English equivalents (eg Field Marshal for *Feldmarschall*, Colonel for
*Oberst*) have also been used, although *Generaloberst* has been left untranslated. People's names,
too, can cause confusion and the same approach has been undertaken with the usual forms
used (eg: Göring, Dönitz with umlauts; but Goebbels without).

**Acknowledgements**

The Introduction was written by Stephen Badsey; the photos came from BPL; the maps
were prepared by Adolofo; thanks to Louise Daubeny for help with the photo choice.

# Contents

# Introduction

## EARLY LIFE 1889-1918

Adolf Hitler's origins were innocent enough; he was not a German—except in the same sense that a Canadian might be called an American. He was born an Austrian citizen and a Roman Catholic at 6.30pm on April 20, 1889, at an inn called the Gasthof zum Pommer in the town of Braunau-am-Inn where his father was Inspector of Customs. When Adolf was three years old his family moved to the town of Passau, where the River Inn joins the Danube. By chance the Austrian customs house at Passau lay within the town on the German side of the border. Consequently, young Adolf grew up speaking German with the characteristic dialect of Bavaria, rather than the cultured accents of Vienna.

Both Hitler's parents were from the farming region about 50 miles north of the Austrian capital. His father, Alois, was born in 1837, the illegitimate child of a peasant girl called Maria Anna Schicklgruber. Five years later, Maria Anna married Johann Georg Hiedler (another spelling of Hitler), but Alois kept the name of Schicklgruber until long after her death. In 1876 Johann Georg acknowledged himself as Alois' father, and he became Alois Hitler. However it is likely that Alois' true father was the man who raised him, Johann Georg's brother, who spelled his name Johann von Nepomuk Hutler. The story that Hitler's real grandfather was Jewish probably has no foundation.

Despite his initial disadvantages, Alois Hitler worked his way up to become a senior civil servant, but his private life was a turbulent one. When his first wife died in 1883 he married his mistress, who was already pregnant with their second child. When she in turn died soon afterwards, he married Klara Pölzl—his second cousin—in January 1885; she was 23 years Alois' junior and also carrying his child. Of their six children only the fourth, Adolf, and the sixth, Paula, survived to adulthood, together with the two children from Alois' previous marriage, Alois and Angela.

In 1895 Alois Hitler retired with his family to live near Linz in upper Austria. It was a grim household; Alois was intensely proud of his customs uniform and of his own rise to upper

*Above:* The church and graveyard in Leonding in Austria contains the grave of Hitler's parents. Hitler spent much of his childhood here, studying at nearby Steyr until he was 16.

*Below:* **The house in Braunau-am-Inn where Adolf Hitler was born on April 20, 1889.**

middle class respectability. He demanded "correct" behavior from his family, reinforced by violent punishments. His elder son, Alois, ran away from home at the age of 14, leaving Adolf as both his chief hope and the target of his rage, while the ineffectual Klara convinced herself that her boy was in poor health and needed constant attention. Adolf was educated at the local village and monastery schools, and when he reached age 11 his father paid for him to attend *Realschule* (secondary school) so that he might also become a civil servant. The young Hitler was not, however, a success. He would later claim that he already wanted to be an artist, and that he deliberately failed his examinations to spite his father. He left school for good in 1905 without having attained the usual leaving certificate.

Alois Hitler died in 1903, leaving his family with enough money to live modestly without the need to work. When his mother—to whom he was devoted—died in 1907, Adolf moved to Vienna, where he had already tried and failed to enter the School of Fine Arts. His artistic talents were more towards draftsmanship than portrait painting, but the School of Architecture would not take him without academic qualifications. After a second rejection by the School of Fine Arts in 1908, he stayed in Vienna, living in hostels and earning his keep by drawing posters for shops and postcard views of the

city for passers-by. Although short of money, he had no responsibilities, nor any pressing need to find steady employment. He mixed with drifters and scroungers, with young idealists, with "bohemians" in both senses of the word. Like many other young men in big cities he was often both poor and lonely, but despite later stories he was never really starving, nor was he ever a house painter.

Hitler's days were spent largely in idle talk; he neither drank nor smoked, and tended towards vegetarianism. He had few friends, being shy and awkward with both men and women, and he could become so violent in argument that others already regarded him as rather strange. He read widely but unsystematically, and in the process became passionate about social issues; he lost whatever remained of his religious faith, replacing it with a vague belief in a Divine Providence. In Vienna his mind was filled with half-formed ideas on politics, philosophy, and culture, a strong and rather tasteless brew from which the poison of his own beliefs was gradually distilled.

Only 20 years before Hitler was born, "Germany" existed only as the dream of the Pan-German movement to recreate the German Empire or Reich that had supposedly existed in Europe in medieval times. The most important German-speaking state was the Austrian Empire, with a majority of non-German subject peoples. Southern Germany was divided into several independent countries of which Bavaria—with Munich as its capital—was the largest. But in the Austro-Prussian War of 1866 Austria was defeated and its power eclipsed by the largely Protestant north German state of Prussia. The weakened Austrian Empire was forced to give Hungary its own internal government as part of the Dual Monarchy of Austria-Hungary. Soon the Slav peoples of Austria-Hungary were also agitating for their own self-government. Prussia and the south German states went on to defeat France—previously the strongest military power in Europe—in the Franco-Prussian War of 1870-71. They then united without Austria into a new German Empire, dominated by Prussia.

The Pan-German idealists, of whom Hitler was one, admired Prussia and the new Germany almost beyond words. In its ruthless ambition and military might it seemed to embody the political philosophies of Friedrich Nietzsche (who finally went mad in the year Hitler was born). Simplified to the level of Vienna café talk, Nietzsche's central creed was that conflict was the chief source of human progress, and that great men should not be bound by conventional ideas of good and evil. The major 19th century advances in biology, particularly Charles Darwin's notion that evolution was due to the competition of species, had also spawned the crank belief that humanity could be physically classified into superior and inferior types. In the

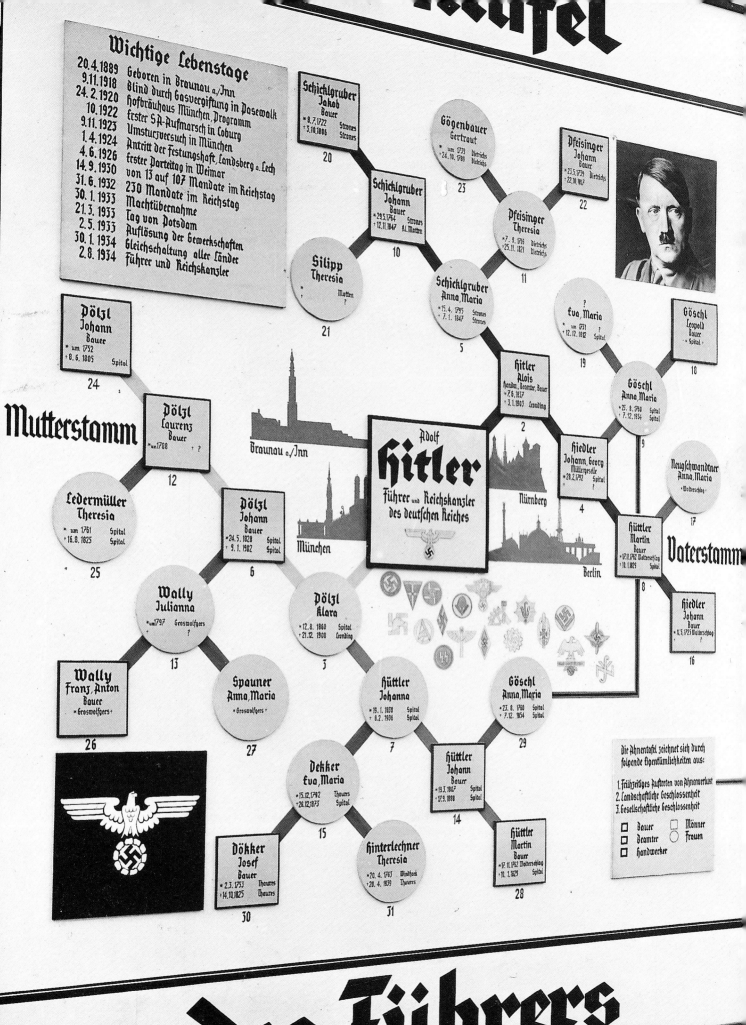

Germanic version that Hitler learned, the *Herrenmenschen* ("Master Race") was represented at its most perfect by the tall, blond, blue-eyed Saxon or Prussian, known due to a ludicrous misunderstanding of prehistory as the "Aryan" type (the real Aryans lived in what is now Iran and Pakistan). Ironically, most of the eventual leaders of Hitler's Nazi Party were Austrians like himself and Adolf Eichmann, Bavarians like Ernst Röhm and Heinrich Himmler, or Rhinelanders like Josef Goebbels and Rudolf Hess.

Although in Hitler's racist view all non-Aryans were *Untermenschen* ("Inferior Races"), Negroes and Asiatics hardly even entered his imagination, which was limited to his own middle European world. Slavs and Czechs he saw as barely human, but he reserved his particular venom for the Jews. In Germany and Austria anti-Semitism had only recently ceased to be "respectable," and was still widely practiced. Successful Jews had risen during the 19th century to positions of importance in industry, finance, and the professions in the major cities, and cosmopolitan Vienna was markedly anti-Semitic (as was Berlin where over one third of Germany's 600,000 Jews lived). In

*Right:* **The classroom in Lembach primary school, Austria, in which Hitler spent his second school year.**

*Below:* **School photograph from Leonding: Hitler is in the middle of the top row.**

Hitler's mind the figure of the Jew became the universal enemy, treacherous, lecherous, and unspeakably evil, the source of all that was corrupt and wicked in the world.

Hitler the politician did not invent this unpleasant and dangerous nonsense; he was invented by it, his political ideas were unoriginal gatherings from the fringe right-wing radical parties of Austria and central Europe. His particular talent was for making the lie both popular and credible. Just as today, most people felt that much in the world was wrong, they admired strength and success, and blamed their misfortunes on others for not being more like themselves. Hitler took the people at their word, and shocked a world that thought it knew where the limits of human evil lay.

In 1913 Hitler moved at last to Germany—Munich—to avoid the risk of conscription in Vienna. He was later judged to be physically unfit for military service, but he was not a coward. When the heir to the Austrian throne, Archduke Franz Ferdinand, was assassinated in Sarajevo on June 28, 1914 by Slav terrorists, World War 1 began. Hitler volunteered for the German Army, joining the 16th Bavarian Reserve Infantry Regiment. He made a very good soldier: for once his life had a purpose and he enjoyed the comradeship, the danger, and the chance to wear uniform. Serving as a company runner on the Western Front throughout the war (except for a short spell in hospital 1916-1917) he won promotion to corporal and two Iron Crosses, one of them the very rare Iron Cross First Class. This

*Left:* **There is no doubting the effect that the carnage of World War 1 had on the participants: but Hitler found comradeship and purpose in the trenches.**

*Below:* **Hitler (second from right, top row) recovering in a field hospital from the gassing he suffered during the battle of Ypres.**

was the happiest time of Hitler's life, and ever afterwards he believed that it had taught him more about the realities of war than his generals ever learned.

Germany fought World War 1 as leader of the Central Powers, including Austria-Hungary, against an alliance led by Great Britain, France, and Imperial Russia. At first the war went well for the Germans, who seized part of northern France and Belgium and held it almost until the end. In November 1917 Russia collapsed in a communist revolution (the "October Revolution" by the Russian calendar) led by V. I. Lenin, whose new government made peace with Germany at Brest-Litovsk in January 1918. This settlement brought into existence something close to the Pan-German ideal of Greater Germany, stretching far eastwards into Russia. After more than three years of war the Germans appeared to be on the verge of total success. But this triumph lasted less than a year. An attempt to starve Great Britain by unrestricted submarine warfare had brought a declaration of war from the United States in April 1917, while in return the British naval blockade produced starvation and riots in German cities. After the failure of its last offensive in the west in spring 1918, the German Army was driven back steadily by the British and French, and by October it had acknowledged defeat. The war ended with armistice on

November 11. The German Emperor, Kaiser Wilhelm II, abdicated and fled the country.

Germany lost World War 1 because the German approach to conflict worked only for short wars against weaker, isolated, opponents. Total war required the complete social, economic, and scientific resources of the country being organized alongside the military effort towards a realistic political aim. As the 19th century German military theorist Karl von Clausewitz put it, "war is the continuation of politics by other means." In Germany by the end of the World War 1 this position had effectively been reversed. The Army Chief of Staff, Field Marshal Paul von Hindenburg, dictated policy to the government, while his deputy, First Quartermaster General E. I. Ludendorff, planned his battles with almost no political objective. Within the German Army, also, absolute priority was given to success on the battlefield; however, it proved to be that German generals were brilliant planners of battles but appallingly bad strategists.

Hitler, who had been temporarily blinded by gas in October 1918, was in hospital when the war ended. His view of war was naive and romantic; to him the defeat of Germany was devastating and incomprehensible. Throughout his life he admired the heroism of the warrior, the power of the general, the flashy uniform, the clever maneuver or technological gimmick, as if war were a game of skill played for its own sake. His hero was the 18th century Prussian warrior-king Frederick the Great. Like many Germans, he could not understand how, with its troops still everywhere on enemy soil, Germany could have lost the war. He grasped at the suggested excuse that the German Army had been "stabbed in the back" by the collapse of political will at home due to Allied propaganda, aided of course by Jewish financiers, left-wing revolutionaries, and traitors. To Hitler, Germany had lost because its leaders had not been ruthless enough, both with the enemy and their own people.

World War 1 ended with the Peace of Versailles in 1919, but in eastern Europe the fighting went on. Germany and Austria-Hungary were in chaos, while Lenin's Russia (renamed the Soviet Union) was committed to extending its revolution. Not until 1923 were the last disputes resolved. The final peace settlement was a mixture of the victorious Allies' desire to punish their enemies, their support for minority races, and democratic ideals, and their conviction that war must never happen again. The League of Nations, a voluntary international organization to settle disputes by peaceful means, was set up in Geneva. The new republics of Austria, Hungary, Czechoslovakia, and Yugoslavia were created from Austria-Hungary. Germany remained precariously intact, but was forced to acknowledge that it had started the war (which was scarcely true), to pay reparations, to endure armies of occupation in the Rhineland, to

*Right:* **One of Hitler's prewar watercolors of Ratzenstadt in the old part of Vienna. He tried to enter the Vienna Fine Arts Academy but was rejected, aged 18, in 1907 while staying with his godparents Johann and Joanna Prinz.**

give up its few overseas colonies, and to reduce its own army to 100,000 men with no tanks or aircraft. The Baltic states of Latvia, Lithuania, and Estonia, together with Poland (which had not existed since 1795) had all fought their way to independence from Russia and in order to give Poland a Baltic port a "corridor" was established through to Danzig (modern Gdansk) cutting off East Prussia from the rest of Germany. Czechoslovakia also received the largely German Sudetenland to use as a defensible frontier. France took back the provinces of Alsace and Lorraine, which had been absorbed into Germany in 1871 together with the largely German Saarland.

By 1918, even the victors were filled with horror at the cost, the suffering, and the waste of the war. Most countries rushed to disband their armed forces and looked to seek security in the League of Nations. The United States went one stage further, refusing to join the League and instead returning to its traditional policy of isolation from world. The British concentrated on their overseas empire, the French, while deeply suspicious of Germany, were unwilling to endure another major war. It seemed impossible that anyone could be so insane as to threaten the world once more with destruction on such a colossal scale.

## RISE TO POWER 1919-1933

After the Kaiser's abdication, Germany became a democratic republic, known as the Weimar Republic from the small town where it was proclaimed. As under the German Empire, the Reichstag (or National Assembly) governed from Berlin, while the old German states, including Bavaria where the king had also abdicated, retained their own assemblies and some degree of internal self-government. Broadly socialist and well-intentioned, the first Weimar government made itself unpopular by accepting the punitive Versailles settlement, and by failing to control the high inflation which followed Germany's defeat and which wiped out savings and led to mass unemployment. By 1922 the German mark was worth a hundredth of its 1918 value against the American dollar. As Germany plunged towards apparent revolution and disintegration, the *Reichswehr* (German Armed Forces) together with unofficial bands of ex-soldiers called *Freikorps*, took an ever greater part in politics. Assassination, intimidation, and murderous street fights became the normal tools of government.

Corporal Hitler returned to Munich in January 1919. He was nearly 30 years old, in poor health, with no friends and no obvious future. In April 1919 the communists proclaimed a Soviet

*Below:* **Early days, early Nazis: a painting of the years of struggle by H. O. Hoyer entitled "In the Beginning was the word."**

*Above:* **The Germany of 1923 endured rampant inflation—even to the extent of having to transport money by wheelbarrow! Economic unrest would help to bring the Nazis to power.**

*Below:* **The SA march past Adolf Hitler on "German Day" in Nuremberg, September 2, 1923. Police estimated that 100,000 people took part in the event**

Republic in Bavaria, only to be crushed by the army and *Freikorps*, which set up a right-wing government. The army put Hitler to work gathering information on revolutionary political groups in Munich. In September 1919, he joined the committee of the tiny *Deutsche Arbeiterpartie* (German Workers' Party), which he had been sent to investigate, and of which his friend Major Ernst Röhm was already a member. In February 1920 the party's name was changed to *Nationalsozialistische Deutsche Arbeiterpartie* or NSDAP, shortened to "Nazi" by its opponents. In April Hitler left the army to concentrate on promoting the Nazi Party, of which he soon became leader. Many of his supporters came from the Bavarian government, from the *Freikorps*, and from the ex-soldiers' association *Stahlhelm* (Steel Helmet).

Like the Weimar government, most European socialists were moderate and democratic, claiming to represent the ordinary man against the aristocracy and big business. Even anti-democratic left-wingers like the communists proclaimed brotherhood with workers in other countries. Some nationalist groups, however, claimed to defend the interests of the German workers while rejecting both internationalism and democracy. This right-wing populism, or "National Socialism," appealed to many Germans who felt that the rest of the world had cheated them

and that Weimar democracy had failed. People like these made up the early membership of the Nazi Party.

Hitler proved brilliant at the seamier side of right-wing politics, which became an outlet for his energies and a substitute for all other passions. He advanced himself and his party with all the skill, determination, and will-power of the true ignorant bigot. Unaccountably, he also turned out to be a public orator of genius. No-one who heard Hitler speak, either to a mass gathering or face to face, ever forgot the experience. He developed a fluent, rhetorical style, full of irony and bathos, which left him physically and emotionally drained after each performance. He had no time for discussion or debate, nor was he particularly good at it. Within a year he was attracting paying audiences in their thousands to Nazi Party meetings, just to hear him speak. The party gained members, including Captain Hermann Göring, a well-known World War 1 fighter ace.

Hitler was intent not only on winning votes but on overthrowing the Weimar Republic by a putsch or violent uprising. In this the Nazis were greatly encouraged by a successful right-wing putsch in Italy in October 1922, when Benito Mussolini, a 37-year old former journalist, marched with his paramilitary forces on Rome and toppled the government. Mussolini called himself *Il Duce* (leader) and his supporters the *Fascisti* or Fascists (from *fasces*, an old Roman symbol of authority). The Nazis copied this shamelessly. Their paramilitary thugs, the SA or *Sturmabteilung* (storm detachment from the shock troops of World War 1) wore brown shirts in imitation of Mussolini's black-shirted Fascists and used their straight-arm salute. Hitler also

*Above:* **A good number of the accused in the trial following the 1923 Beer Hall Putsch are shown here. From left to right: 1 Pernet, 2 Dr. Weber, 3 Wilhelm Frick, 4 Griebe, 5 General Erich Ludendorff, 6 Hitler, 7 Brückner, 8 Ernst Röhm, 9 Wagner.**

*Above:* **Hitler's release from Landsberg prison, December 20, 1924. Photograph taken by Heinrich Hoffmann, his photographer and the man who introduced Hitler to Eva Braun.**

called himself leader—*Führer.* The Nazi swastika, an ancient Aryan symbol, came from another nationalist party.

In January 1923, in response to the Weimar government's failure to keep up reparations' payments, French troops occupied the Ruhr, Germany's industrial heartland, and the German economy collapsed. From 400 marks to the dollar in 1922, there were 7,000 by February 1923, 160,000 by July, 1,000,000 by August and 130,000,000,000 by November. In Berlin and Munich a state of emergency was declared. Hitler saw this as his chance. His first attempt at a putsch in Munich on May 1 was a damp squib, but on November 8-9 he tried again, this time with a respectable figurehead, the former First Quartermaster General Erich Ludendorff. The "Beer Hall Putsch" (mounted from the Bürgerbräukeller, the biggest beer hall in Munich) fell apart when a march by about 3,000 SA brownshirts led by Hitler and Ludendorff was fired on by police. The leaders of the putsch were arrested, while other participants such as Göring—who was wounded in the shooting—fled the country.

At the trial, Ludendorff was acquitted on a technicality, while the unsavory nature of Bavarian politics led to Hitler, who turned the court into a political circus, receiving the minimum possible sentence of five years. He served just under nine months of comfortable confinement in Landsberg Fortress, using the opportunity to dictate his political memoirs, *Mein Kampf* (My Struggle), to the young Rudolf Hess. It is hard to say how far this book constituted a real political program; later, when trying to

*Below:* **Garden of the Landsberg Prison, Bavaria, where Hitler served his sentence for his part in the 1923 Munich Putsch.**

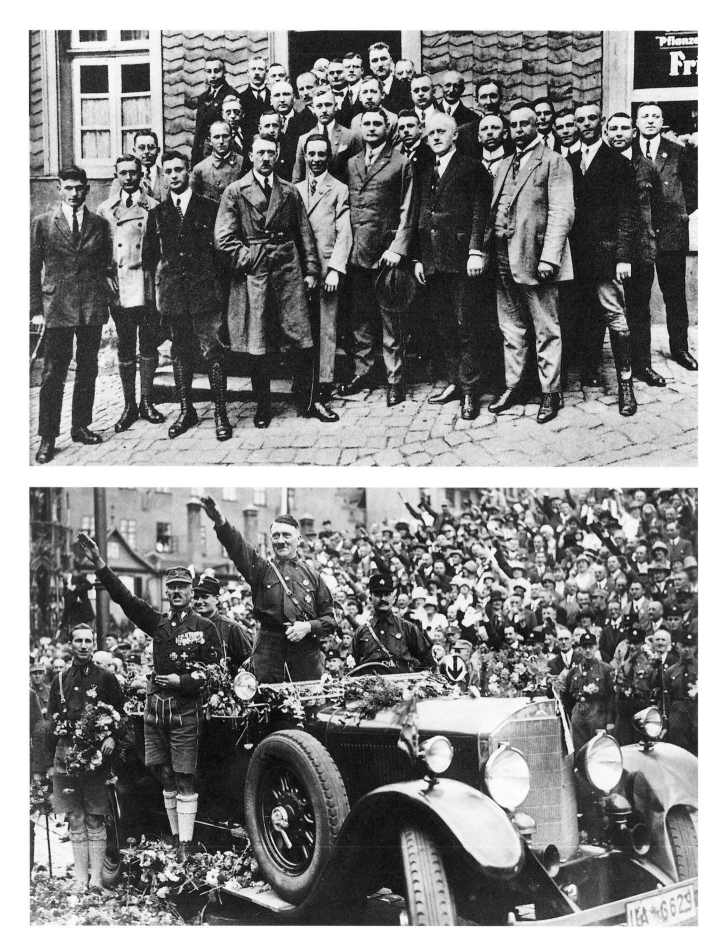

*Above left:* **The core of the Nazis begins to coalesce around Hitler. Here in 1926 he is pictured with Goebbels, who had originally been affiliated to Streicher. Two rows behind Goebbels is Viktor Lutze, who succeeded Ernst Röhm as head of the SA after the June 30, 1934 Blood Purge. They are on the steps of the Märker guest house after meeting Nazi party supporters in Hattinger.**

*Left:* **NSDAP Party rally in Nuremberg, August 19/20, 1927. To Hitler's right are: Hess, Captain Franz Felix Pfeffer von Saloman, early leader of the SA, and Georg Halbermann.**

*Above:* **Another view of Nuremberg 1927: from left of photograph: Himmler, Hess, Gregor Strasser, Hitler, von Saloman.**

appear a respectable statesman, Hitler wished that he had never written it. In *Mein Kampf* he argued for war in the east to create a "Greater Germany"—*Grossdeutschland*—at the expense of the Soviet Union. The book also reaffirmed all Hitler's hatreds, especially against the Jews, and against the communists whom he saw as part of the Jewish conspiracy. *Mein Kampf* sold over 300,000 copies before 1933, enabling Hitler to live on the proceeds.

On his release Hitler was banned from public speaking and the Nazi Party briefly outlawed. Hitler refounded the party in February 1925 with a membership of fewer than 30,000. In February 1926 he did deals to win the support of his chief rivals for the Nazi leadership, Josef Goebbels and Gregor Strasser. Goebbels proved unusually gifted at organizing publicity, and with his backing Hitler once more began to attract wider interest. In 1927 (the year that Göring returned to Germany) the *Hitler Jugend* (Hitler Youth) was founded and the first mass rally held at Nuremberg. A year later, Hitler put Goebbels in full charge of Nazi propaganda.

When the Weimar president, Friedrich Ebert, died in 1925, the Nazis put up Ludendorff as a candidate, but withdrew their support when a better alternative presented itself in Ludendorff's former commander, Field Marshal Paul von Hindenburg, who became president with the support of almost

*Right:* **By 1929 the** *Parteitage*—**party days—at Nuremberg had become massive events. Held over August 2-5, the 1929 Nuremberg Rally spread throughout the city and all its open spaces. Here at the Luitpoldhain, Hitler is saluted by Standartenführer Warzbacker.**

*Below:* **Hitler with General Franz Ritter von Epp, right-wing commander of a** *Freikorps* **unit and an early supporter of Hitler. Von Epp would command the SA in Bavaria and represent Upper Bavaria-Swabia in the Reichstag in 1928.**

*Below right*: **Hitler at the 1929 Nuremberg Rally: behind, to the right of the photograph, is Viktor Lutze.**

*Above:* **Hitler is driven through the streets of Weimar during a National Socialist Rally in 1930.**

*Below:* **Hitler at the *Braunes Haus* (Brown House), Munich, in 1930 at the inauguration of building work. Behind him in civilian clothes is Julius Schaub, his adjutant. The old Barlow "Palace" (a large house) at Briennerstrasse 45 became the *Braunes Haus* and the Nazi Party Headquarters from 1931, after having been rebuilt to the design of Paul Ludwig Troost working to Hitler's directions.**

all the nationalist parties. With von Hindenburg as a figurehead, the German economy began temporarily to recover. Inflation eased, the problem of reparations was solved by international agreement, average wages rose, and in 1928 unemployment dropped back to one million for the first time in some years. Meanwhile, Germany was accepted back into the international community and was allowed to join the League of Nations in 1926. Two years later Germany became one of 65 countries to sign the Kellogg-Briand Pact, renouncing war as an instrument of policy; and in 1930, on condition that no German troops were ever stationed in the Rhineland, the last French soldiers left German soil.

After the Beer Hall Putsch, Hitler accepted that politics rather than force was the way to power. This meant doing deals with the other nationalist parties, with big business, with the landowners and agricultural lobby, and not forgetting the army. It also meant giving up the Nazi Party's revolutionary past and brutal image. The SA, although still valuable for street fights and intimidation, was too independent and devoted to the putsch to suit Hitler's new style. In 1928 he appointed Heinrich Himmler—an almost pathologically loyal SA member—to head his small personal bodyguard, the black-shirted SS (*Schutzstaffel*—lit: defense echelon), which Himmler developed

into Hitler's private army. Hitler also convinced Röhm, who had emigrated, to return to Germany in 1930 and take over command of the SA for him.

However there was a problem in the way of Hitler's ambitions: he was not a German citizen, and thus could not run for office in Germany. He solved the problem by renouncing his Austrian citizenship in 1925 leaving himself legally stateless, and in 1928 he moved from Munich to Berchtesgaden in the Bavarian Alps, where his elder sister Angela kept house for him. (He would solve his citizenship problem only in 1932, just before he stood for the presidency: on February 25, 1932, the Minister of the Interior of Brunswick—a Nazi—announced that Hitler was an attaché of the Brunswick legation at Berlin. This made Hitler immediately a citizen of Brunswick and, therefore, of Germany too.)

In Berchtesgaden, at nearly 40 years of age, Hitler fell in love with his niece, Angela's elder daughter, Geli Raubal. The relationship proved a difficult one, and she was found shot dead, almost certainly suicide, two years later. Shortly afterwards Hitler struck up a relationship with Eva Braun, an employee of Heinrich Hoffmann, Hitler's photographer. She became his mistress and took over the running of his house in 1936. Hitler liked the company of women, of children, and of dogs. He seems to have tolerated rather than indulged the strong homosexual element within the Nazi Party, which included Röhm. His private weaknesses, apart from a growing hypochondria, were for chocolate cake, pulp westerns, and Wagner; otherwise, politics and power consumed his life.

As Germany prospered, support for the Nazis dwindled almost to nothing. Membership stood in 1928 at 108,000, but in the May elections the party polled only 2.5 percent of the vote, losing 20 of its 32 seats in the Reichstag. Even the communists did better with 54 seats. Hitler's chance came with the Wall Street Crash of October 1929, which plunged the world into a deep depression. The Weimar economy depended heavily on overseas loans, and by December there were two million Germans out of work. In March 1930 the coalition government fell apart, and the chancellor, Hermann Müller, was granted emergency powers by von Hindenburg to rule by direct decree. In September his successor, Heinrich Brüning, called an election in the hope of winning an outright majority. By now, the Nazis looked increasingly attractive both to ordinary voters and to industrial magnates afraid of Communism and the trade unions. With financial backing from these industrialists, the Nazis took a third of the electoral votes, and 107 out of 491 Reichstag seats.

Brüning continued to rule by decree and with the support of the socialist parties, who saw him as a lesser threat than Hitler.

But as the depression deepened, German banking houses failed, and at the end of 1931 over six million people—one quarter of the German workforce—were unemployed. Street battles between the SA and paramilitary groups from other parties, the communist *Rotfrontkämpferbund* (Red Front Fighters' Association) and the Social Democrats' *Reichsbanner*, became commonplace. In the first half of 1931 over 200 political murders took place in public. The army, faced once more with the prospect of keeping order, also began to take Hitler seriously. In March 1932 Hitler stood against von Hindenburg as president. Contriving to make even the 84-year old "father of Germany" look unpatriotic for supporting Brüning, Hitler forced the election to a second ballot. Von Hindenburg won with 19,250,000 votes, but an impressive 13,500,000 votes went to Hitler.

Brüning could not survive this; in June, after trying to ban the Nazi SA brownshirts (now 300,000 strong) he was brought down by an alliance of nationalist politicians, landowners, army officers, and industrialists orchestrated by the new Defense Minister, General Kurt von Schleicher, who put in his place the right-wing Catholic Franz von Papen. The situation was perfect for the gutter politics at which Hitler excelled, this time with Germany itself as the prize. It was a shameful position for a great country to be in, and it produced a shameful result. The ban on the brownshirts was lifted, and in the July elections the Nazis secured over 37 percent of the vote and 230 seats as the largest single party in the Reichstag.

*Above:* **Laying of the foundation stone for the National Memorial to composer Richard Wagner in Leipzig on March 6, 1931. From the left: Winifred Wagner, Hitler, Chief Mayor Dr. Goerdeler, Martin Mutschmann Gauleiter of Saxony, Josef Goebbels.**

*Above right:* **Hitler and Lutze in Brunswick, February 1931. Lutze represented Hanover-Brunswick in the Reichstag for the Nazis.**

*Right:* **The convention held at Bad Harzburg in October 1931 saw the Harzburg Front mooted: an alliance of nationalists against the government of Chancellor Heinrich Brüning. Hitler's support for the alliance was lukewarm as he thought it would restrict his party. The picture shows Hitler leaving the convention with, to his left, Brückner (hidden), Schaub, and Hess.**

*Far right:* **Hitler addresses an audience in Berlin's *Lustgarten* (Pleasure Gardens) during the presidential elections on April 4, 1932. Wilhelm Brückner, his adjutant, is on Hitler's left.**

*Previous page:* **Hitler during the District Party Rally in Weimar, October 1930.**

Refused the chancellorship by von Schleicher and von Papen, Hitler proceeded to wreck the workings of the Reichstag, aided by Göring as Speaker. Like his predecessors, von Papen governed briefly by decree, and in November called another election. The Nazis did worse than before with 196 seats, but still remained the largest single party. In December, von Schleicher himself took over as chancellor from von Papen, trying to split the Nazis by offering Gregor Strasser the vice-chancellorship. At this first major political crisis of his career, Hitler kept his grip and his nerve. Meanwhile von Papen, backed by the leading industrialists, attempted to return to power. Convinced that he could control Hitler, he persuaded the nearly senile von Hindenburg to give Hitler what he wanted, the chancellorship, as part of a nationalist coalition. On January 30, 1933 von Hindenburg appointed Hitler Chancellor of Germany.

Under the Weimar constitution, Hitler's appointment was perfectly legal and proper, no matter what his supporters were doing on the streets. As part of the agreement with von Papen his new cabinet contained only three Nazis out of 12 members. Von Papen himself became vice-chancellor, and Minister-President of Prussia with Göring as his interior minister. New elections were set for March 5, and there were hopes that Nazi support would decline as before. Then, on the evening of

February 27, a fire broke out in the Reichstag building and it burned to the ground. A Dutchman called Marinus van der Lubbe was arrested and tried for starting the fire; he claimed to have acted on his own.

How the Reichstag fire really started still remains a mystery. Hitler and the Nazis portrayed it as the start of a communist uprising to topple the state. On the following morning, von Hindenburg signed a declaration allowing the government emergency powers of arrest. Göring, who had already packed the Prussian police force with Nazis, deputized 25,000 SA brownshirts and 15,000 SS stormtroopers as auxiliary policemen, and rounded up communists, socialists, and other enemies of the Nazi party. The March 5 elections took place amid an atmosphere of confusion, hysteria, terror, and violence. Altogether 89 percent of the electorate voted, and the Nazis received 44 percent of these votes, or 17,300,000, giving Hitler 288 out of 647 Reichstag seats—not quite enough for an outright majority. Hitler overcame this shortfall by a quick deal with the 52 Catholic Center Party deputies, and by declaring the election of 81 communists invalid. On March 23, after solemn promises of good behavior by Hitler, the Reichstag passed by 441 to 94 votes an "Enabling Act," allowing him to govern by decree for four years, and including the right to change the constitution. The Reichstag never met again: Hitler had taken control of Germany and would not relinquish power until his death 12 years later.

*Right:* **Hitler at a youth rally in Potsdam on October 2, 1932. In front of him, to the right, is Baldur von Schirach, whom Hitler had made Reich youth leader of the NSDAP in 1931.**

*Below right:* **Poster carriers in front of a polling station in Berlin during the presidential elections of April 10, 1932. Hitler won 30 percent of the vote, but Paul von Hindenburg retained his position as president: within 10 months he would make Hitler chancellor.**

*Below:* **A key moment in Nazi internal politics: the last National Socialist Parliamentary Party meeting in which Gregor Strasser (to the left of Hitler) took part. At odds with Hitler for some years, Strasser resigned his party positions on December 8, 1932. He would die in the 1934 Blood Purge. On Hitler's right is the President/Chairman of the National Socialist Parliamentary Party, Dr. Wilhelm Frick.**

# 1933

The German elections of November 1932 had seen the Nazi Party lose seats in the Reichstag and Hitler could no longer be guaranteed an overall majority even in coalition with the nationalists. However, he continued to demand that he be given the position of chancellor, believing that he could strike a bargain with various elements of the old establishment, including the army, that would allow him to take up the position. In early January Hitler's fortunes took a turn for the better, chiefly due to the intervention of Franz von Papen.

Accompanied by Rudolf Hess, Heinrich Himmler, and Wilhelm Keppler, a pro-Nazi industrialist, Hitler traveled to Cologne in great secrecy. They met von Papen on January 4 in the home of a banker, Kurt von Schröder. The meeting lasted two hours and Papen suggested an alliance between his nationalists and the Nazi Party, with the two of them becoming joint chancellors. Hitler responded by saying that if he was chancellor he would also have to be head of state, but he was willing to allow nationalists as members of his cabinet. The meeting did not settle the issue of coalition but laid the foundations for one.

After the meeting, Hitler threw himself into electioneering in the state of Lippe. Accompanied by Goebbels, he stayed in Vinsebeck castle and traveled widely from there giving speeches, whipping up support for the Nazi Party. The elections on January 15 saw the Nazis win nearly 40 percent of the vote.

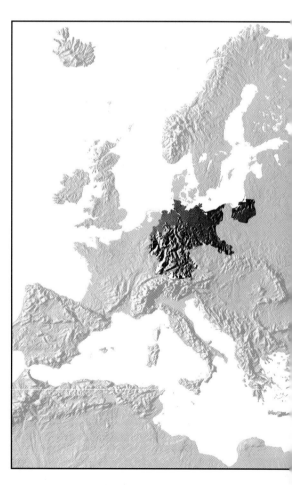

*Above:* **President Paul von Hindenburg and Chancellor Adolf Hitler pictured during the 19th anniversary celebrations of the German victory over the Russians at Tannenberg in 1914.**

*Below left:* **Germany's boundaries at the end of 1933.**

*Below:* **January 22, 1933: at the grave in Berlin of Horst Wessel, a young SA recruit who wrote** *Die Fahne Hoch* **(Raise the Flag High) reputedly killed in street fighting with communists in 1930. Amongst others, from the left: Secretary of State Karl Hanke, in civilian clothes with a beard; Count Wolf Heinrich von Helldorf, leader of the SA in Berlin; Wilhelm Brückner, Hitler's adjutant; Hitler; Ernst Röhm, head of the SA; Goebbels.**

Hitler then returned to Berlin to continue his efforts to convince the public and the conservative old guard that the Nazis were a force to be reckoned with. On the 22nd, Hitler spoke to over 10,000 members of the SA who had provocatively marched by the headquarters of the Communist Party.

Hitler finally gained upper hand over the nationalists and got agreement to his taking over the position of chancellor on January 22. During the evening Hitler attended a meeting at Joachim von Ribbentrop's home at Dahlem. Also present were Göring, Frick, von Papen, Otto Meissener and the president's son, Oskar von Hindenburg. During the morning of the 30th Hitler received a summons to meet with President Hindenburg. He left the Kaiserhof and traveled to the Reichs Chancellery. A little time after midday, Hitler announced to his Nazi Party officials that he had been made chancellor. It was a momentous occasion. Members of the old political and military establishment believed they could control the brash corporal but, as events over the next few months were to prove, it was Hitler who would move more effectively consolidate his position.

On the afternoon of the 30th Hitler attended his first cabinet meeting. He made it plain that if, as he intended, a viable coalition could not be formed, he intended to dissolve the Reichstag and hold elections as soon as possible. As chancellor, Hitler

*Above:* **Hitler pictured shortly after the Reichstag fire of February 27, 1933. Next to him is Prince August William of Prussia; to his right is Hermann Göring, President of the Reichstag, in conversation with a police officer.**

controlled much of the state apparatus and would have an enormous advantage over other political parties in the hustings. A date for the elections was fixed and Hitler threw all his energies into the campaign, traveling the length and breadth of Germany.

However, before the electioneering went into full swing Hitler needed to reassure the army that he had no intention of undermining its authority and pre-eminent position in Germany. At a meeting on February 2, held at the home of the army commander-in-chief, Kurt von Hammerstein-Equord, Hitler spoke to the assembled high-ranking officers for close to two hours. He was at pains to stress his commitment to expanding and rearming the armed forces and that he expected the army would stand outside any political unrest. His words were ideally suited to the army's concerns and, with the forces placated, Hitler turned his attention to the forthcoming elections. He needed to suggest that he had a radical political vision, one much more dynamic that those of other parties. Equally he had to be careful not to isolate himself from industrialists and the army.

*Above:* **Starting to build the German *Autobahn* system—motorways—Hitler inspects work for the Frankfurt Autobahn, September 23, 1933.**

*Below:* **Magda Goebbels leaves the polling station, March 5, 1933. At the elections the Nazis would poll 44 percent of the vote and gain 288 seats in the Reichstag.**

At Kassel on February 11 he spoke out against the weakness of rival political parties: "They have had no program. Now it is too late for their plans, the time for their ideas is past. The period of international phrases is over and its place will be taken by the solidarity of the German people. No one in the world will help us—only ourselves." Hitler, however, was careful to avoid making explicit just what the Nazi Party's manifesto contained. He wished to avoid antagonizing the country's industrialists and armed forces. At a speech in Munich on the 24th he said: "Programs are of no avail, it is the human purpose which is decisive. The first point in our program is: away with all illusions." Between these meetings Hitler addressed a small gathering of leading industrialists in Berlin on the 20th. "Now we stand before the last election. Whatever the outcome, there will be no retreat. One way or another, if the election does not decide, the decision must be brought about by other means." Whether cowed by Hitler's thinly veiled threats or eager to make money out of rearmament, the industrialists agreed to fund much of the Nazis' election costs.

An event now occurred that had all the hallmarks of Hitler's backstreet politics, although it might well have not involved the Nazis. Whatever the truth of the matter, the Reichstag in Berlin was burned down on the 27th, probably by a communist,

Deutsche, verteidigt Euch
gegen die jüdische
Greuelpropaganda,
kauft
nur bei Deutschen!
Germans defend
yourselves against jewish
atrocity propaganda
buy only at German shops!
Deutsche!
Wehrt Euch!
Kauft nicht bei Juden!

*Left:* Anti-Semitism grows with Nazi boycotts of Jewish shops. An SA post in front of a Jewish shop in Berlin, April 1, 1933.

*Below:* Röhm, Hitler, Franz Seldte, who was joint founder of the right-wing *Stahlhelm*—an ex-servicemen's association—and Minister of Defense Werner von Blomberg take a salute, Berlin, September 23-24, 1933.

Marianus van der Lubbe. Hitler immediately used the arson attack to strike against the German communists. The following day a decree was announced that ended the right of individual liberty. Other clauses allowed the central government to take over the powers exercised by individual states and introduced draconian new penalties for high treason, poisoning, arson, and sabotage. Hitler would go on to use these new laws against his political opponents.

On March 4 Hitler addressed a rally in Königsberg: "German people, hold your heads high and proudly once more. You are no longer enslaved and in bondage, but you are free again." The speech marked the conclusion of the election race. Hitler won slightly less than 44 percent of the votes, sufficient to form a minority government. With other nationalist parties he had a working majority. In the months following his election victory, Hitler moved to secure his position. The army was again courted and he was able to push through the Reichstag, now meeting in Berlin's Kroll Opera House, a series of laws that would sweep away all of his political opponents.

*Left:* **Hitler's 1933 cabinet—from the left: Walter Funk, Dr. Hans Lammers, Richard-Walther Darré, Franz Seldte, Franz Gürtner, Josef Goebbels, Paul von Eltz-Rühenach, Hitler, Göring, ?, Werner von Blomberg, Dr. Wilhelm Frick, Constantin von Neurath, Dr. Hjalmar Schacht, Lutz Graf Schwerin von Krosigk, Johannes Popitz, Franz von Papen, Otto Meissner.**

*Below left:* **Hitler commemorates the 10th Anniversary of the Beer Hall Putsch in Munich by remembering those who died on November 9, 1923—16 Nazis and three policemen.**

*Below:* **Another commemoration of the 10th Anniversary of the 1923 Munich Beer Hall Putsch. Hitler parades with the *Alte Kämpfer—* the Nazi old guard; also present is Julius Streicher (holding flag).**

Hitler also intended to spread belief in Nazism throughout Germany. To this end, he at first turned to the SA, who had been at the vanguard of the movement's successes. At a meeting in Kiel on May 7 he said: "You have carried this revolution to victory. You must be the guarantors of the victorious completion of this revolution, and it will be victoriously completed only if through your school a new German people is educated." This was a theme that Hitler returned to on June 14, when he addressed a meeting of senior Nazis: "Its [the National Socialist "revolution"] dynamic force still dominates development in Germany today, a development which presses forward irresistibly to a complete remodeling of German life."

Hitler was, however, no revolutionary and was unwilling to press the remodeling too far. The SA and its leader, Ernst Röhm, wanted greater change and many were concerned over Hitler's attempts to support the old army establishment and the country's leading businessmen, whom the SA saw as representatives of the existing order that Hitler had promised to sweep away. Hitler initially attempted to placate the SA leadership but it quickly became clear that he could not. The problem dominated Hitler's thinking for the second half of 1933, but the problem would not be resolved until the summer of 1934.

# GERMANY IN 1933

Germany in 1933 was a country waiting for something to happen. Crushed by the treaty of Versailles, rampant inflation, and lack of a strong traditional political presence, it was ripe for Hitler and the Nazis. Although there were opposition parties aplenty, and strong support for them, there was no one other than Hitler with the political will, self belief, and popular agenda. It took only two years for a totalitarian government completely to take over the government and instruments of governing Germany: the Nazis would not let them go again until the country had been brought to its knees.

*Right:* Hitler at the window of the Chancellery in Berlin's Wilhelmstrasse during the evening of January 30, 1933, the day he became chancellor.

*Below:* The Hitler Jugend hadn't started wearing brown shirts in 1933, but they and the whole of Germany awaited the future expectantly.

# 1934

During Hitler's second year in office he concentrated his efforts in three key areas. First, he extended his control over the various offices of the state. Second, he eliminated those members of the old Nazi hierarchy who might threaten him or disagreed with his vision of Nazism. Third, Hitler began to plot the extension of the territory controlled by the Third Reich. He made his first major moves on the international stage. On January 26, it was announced that Germany had signed a Non-Aggression Pact with Poland. Hitler knew that it would be unpopular with the public but he knew that he could not challenge Poland until Germany was rearmed. On the 30th he explained to the Reichstag in Berlin his motive for concluding the treaty: "Germans and Poles will have to learn to accept the fact of each other's existence in such a way that the highest possible profit will accrue from it for both nations."

In the first months of 1934 Hitler also completed the political reorganization of Germany. On the day of the Reichstag speech, the Law for the Restoration of the Reich confirmed the supremacy of central government over the offices of the individual federal states. In a speech on March 22 Hitler outlined his view of the role of the Third Reich: "National Socialism has as its historic task to create the new Reich and not to preserve the German states."

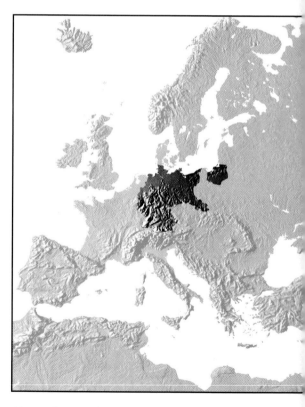

*Above:* **Germany's boundaries at end of 1934.**

*Right:* **Hitler addresses a mass gathering of Hitler Youth at Nuremberg in September 1934.**

In the spring of 1934 Hitler became increasingly concerned about the political power of the SA and resolved to bring the organization to heel. For this he needed to placate the senior generals of the armed forces. During a short cruise out from Kiel on the warship *Deutschland* on April 11, Hitler met Minister of Defense Werner von Blomberg, Werner von Fritsch, the commander of the German army, and Admiral Eric Raeder, head of the navy. Hitler made it plain that he would deal with the SA and its leadership, and maintain the army as the country's chief defense force if it would back him as German's leader. This was later agreed to.

Hitler also intended to destroy the German trade union movement. To offset the fear of trade unionists, he held a May Day Rally in Berlin at which he expressed support for the movement. However, the next day the SA and SS took over trade union offices throughout the country, arresting many leading activists, and a new German Labor Front was founded. On May 10 Hitler addressed the First Congress of Nazi Workers. He spoke of the importance of labor and his desire to end the friction between capital and the workers. However, by the end of the month a new law ordered the setting up of government figures who would be responsible for workers' conditions and pay bargaining.

Hitler's main preoccupation during the following months was the SA and its leader, Ernst Röhm. The SA, with a strength of

*Left:* **Hitler is greeted by President Paul von Hindenburg before a service of remembrance for the fallen of World War 1. Behind Hitler from the right: Raeder (head of the German Navy), Göring, Werner von Fritsch (army commander-in-chief), Minister of Defense Werner von Blomberg's arm. Behind Hindenburg, half hidden, his son Oskar.**

*Below left:* **The reorganization of society that accompanied the Nazis' seizure of power was called** *Gleichschaltung.* **On May 1, 1934 a rally was held to celebrate and here Hitler arrives at the major parade of SA and SS at Tempelhofer Feld in Berlin. Tempelhof was once Germany's largest airport and was the main location for Allied supply aircraft during the postwar Berlin airlift.**

*Below:* **Before the laying of the foundation stone of the newly built Reichs Bank in Berlin on May 5, 1934. Hitler, accompanied by President of the Reichs Bank, Dr Hjalmar Schacht, sets off for the celebrations.**

*Below right:* **A photograph of the VIP box in the Dresden Opera House, on the opening of the German Theatre's Festival Week, May 27, 1934.**

more that 500,000 members, was chiefly concerned with economic rather than political change. As such, they claimed to represent the early, true character of Nazism. They also wanted to remain the only "military" defense force and believed that the army should remain nothing more than a training cadre. Under the promptings of his closest advisers, Hitler decide to destroy the SA leadership. On June 4 Hitler met Röhm and the two spoke for more than five hours, with Hitler asking him to rein in the SA and pull back from any challenge to his authority. A little later it was announced that the SA was to go on leave for the whole of July. Röhm, however, issued a public memo stating that: "If the foes of the SA are nursing the hope that the SA will not return from their leave, we are ready to let them enjoy this hope for a short time. The SA is, and remains, Germany's destiny." Röhm had signed his own death warrant.

While the SA was resting, Hitler made his first visit to Italy to meet Benito Mussolini in Venice. The Italian trip, Hitler's first foreign mission since he had become chancellor, began on June 14 but Hitler was forced to play second fiddle to Mussolini. Hitler's mood was not improved by a speech given on June 17 by his vice-chancellor, Franz von Papen, who openly criticized Hitler's style of government and his policies. Hitler responded

*Left:* **Hitler and Mussolini in Venice, June 1934; this was Hitler's first foreign visit since becoming chancellor.**

*Below:* **From the left: Wilhelm Brückner and Julius Schaub, two of Hitler's adjutants; Hitler, Martin Bormann, Adolf Wagner—the Gauleiter of Upper Bavaria—and Interior Minister Dr. Wilhelm Frick. Photo taken Munich c. 1934.**

to von Papen's speech while visiting Gera in Thuringia. He was highly critical, brushing aside the criticisms of "the pygmy who imagines he can stop with a few phrases the gigantic renewal of a people's life." Hitler met von Papen on the 20th and the vice-chancellor made it clear that he and other members of the cabinet, representatives of the old conservative order, were close to resignation.

Hitler needed to discover the position of the ailing president, Paul von Hindenburg, so flew to Neudeck on the 21st. There he also met von Blomberg, who, with the president's backing, reminded Hitler of their agreement to make the regular armed forces Germany's only legitimate defense force. To keep the generals and his cabinet from deserting him, Hitler had to act quickly. On June 28 Hitler left Berlin for Essen, where he was to be present at the wedding of a local political leader, Josef Terboven. Back in Berlin, Heinrich Himmler, head of the SS, and Herman Göring, Prussian Minister of the Interior, ordered their forces to prepare to strike against Röhm and the SA. On the following day Hitler visited a number of labor camps in Westphalia and spent the afternoon and part of the evening at Bad Godesberg on the Rhine. During the evening He met Goebbels, Otto Dietrich—the Nazi Party's press chief—and Viktor Lutze, SA-Obergruppenführer of Hanover and loyal to Hitler. Lutze

agreed to take Röhm's position. The final decision to deal with Röhm was made.

From Godesberg, early in the morning of the 30th, Hitler, Goebbels, and Lutze flew by plane to Munich and the so-called "Blood Purge," the purge of Röhm and the SA, had begun. SA members were killed outright or taken prisoner throughout Germany. Röhm was at Wiessee outside Munich. He was taken back to Munich's Stadelheim Prison and shot at close range by two SS officers. Gregor Strasser, another SA leader, was captured in Berlin and executed almost immediately at one of the capital's prisons on Prinz Albrechtstrasse. Von Papen escaped with his life but was kept under house arrest for a few days. Hitler returned to Berlin from Munich late on the evening of June 30, where he was met at Tempelhof airport by Göring, Himmler, and Wilhelm Frick, Reichs Minister of the Interior. The following day, while the executions continued, Hitler gave a tea party in the grounds of the Reichs Chancellery. Hitler received the thanks of the president, Hindenburg, and von Blomberg.

Hitler appeared before the Reichstag on July 13 to explain the destruction of the SA. He laid the blame for the recent events squarely on the shoulders of Röhm and the SA leadership, highlighting their corruption. He then argued that they

*Below:* **Hitler and Foreign Minister Constantin von Neurath during the burial of Karin, wife of Hermann Göring, June 19, 1934.**

*Right:* **Hitler and (to his left) Baldur von Schirach study the progress of the rebuilding of the** *Braunes Haus* **in Munich, August 30, 1934.**

wanted revolution not for the benefit of Germany but for their own benefit. Frick constructed a post facto law which declared all Hitler's actions during the Blood Purge to be legal. The tame Reichstag passed it without demure.

On August 2 Hindenburg died and Hitler immediately consolidated his position as unchallenged head of the Third Reich. It was announced that the position of president would be merged with than of chancellor. Hitler became the head of state and commander-in-chief of the country's armed forces. The army was to swear a new oath of allegiance, not to Germany but to Hitler. Hitler gave a memorial address to the Reichstag in Berlin on the 6th and then attended Hindenburg's funeral.

On September 5 Hitler, whose position had been immeasurably strengthened by the events of the previous months, attempted to reassure the assembled masses at Nuremberg that the recent upheavals were a thing of the past: "Just as the world cannot live on wars, so peoples cannot live on revolutions. Revolutions have always been rare in Germany. The age of nerves of the 19th century has found its close with us. In the next thousand years there will be no other revolution in Germany." Hitler was also keen to reassure the wider world of his peaceful intentions. At a meeting with a French politician in November, Hitler spoke of his horror of conflict: "We know too well you and I the uselessness and horror of war." The following year, however, Hitler would attempt to break free of the impositions placed on Germany by the Treaty of Versailles and the process of rearmament, which was explicitly prohibited by Versailles, would gather pace.

# MEETING THE PEOPLE

*Right:* Girls from the Austrian BDM (*Bund Deutscher Mädel*) with Hitler.

*Below:* Hitler and Hess are greeted by a member of the Hitler Youth, which—along with the female version, the *Bund Deutscher Mädel*—was a state organisation designed to create a stream of perfect young National Socialists. The Hitler Youth took children from the age of 14 to 18—they would go on from there to the *Reichsarbeitdienst* (State Labor Service) and then the Wehrmacht (German Armed Forces).

*Below right:* As with all politicians, photo opportunities with children were an important part of Hitler's prewar life.

*Above:* "Enraptured young people."

*Right:* Hitler Youth in Berchtesgaden for the corner stone laying of a youth common lodging house on April 20, 1935, Hitler's birthday.

# 1935

Hitler began 1935 with a political coup that greatly increased his prestige with the German people. On January 13, the ethnic Germans living in the Saarland voted overwhelming to reunite with Germany. The Saarland, a rich industrial region, had been placed under the control of the League of Nations for 15 years as part of the Treaty of Versailles. It was actually administered by France, which had been permitted to exploit its resources. Three days later, on the 16th, during an interview with the American journalist Pierre Huss at Obersalzberg, Hitler was able to boast that one of the great injustices enforced on Germany by Versailles had been swept away. On March 1, the day that the Saarland was formally returned to Germany, Hitler, along with German Werner von Fritsch, the commander-in-chief of the army, traveled to Saarbrücken to view a celebratory parade by army units

Hitler also aimed to sweep away the restrictions on the strength of the German armed forces that had been a key part of the World War 1 armistice treaty. Germany had been rearming for some time and could no longer hide the fact. Hitler decided to force the issue; on March 9 the existence of a German air force was announced and a week later it was declared that conscription was to be reintroduced and the army greatly expanded. On March 17, Heroes' Remembrance Day, Hitler attended a lavish military event at Berlin's State Opera

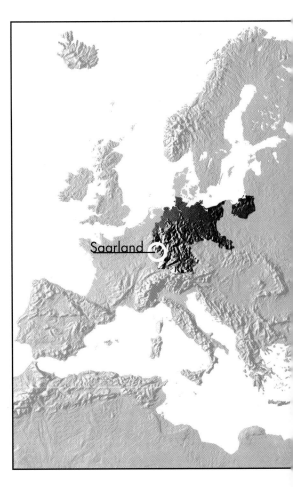

Saarland

*Above:* **Hitler attends a parade of Hitler Youth marines in Worms with Gauleiter Sprenger of Hesse-Nassau.**

*Below left:* **Germany's boundaries at end 1935.**

*Below:* **Hitler and Göring, along with the French ambassador in Berlin, André François-Poncet (centre), view a stand at an automobile exhibition at the Kaiserdamm, Berlin. Behind Hitler is Major Adolf Hühnlein, head of the NSKK, the Nazi Motor Corps.**

House. The event was organized to celebrate the expansion of the army. Hitler was accompanied by Field Marshal August von Mackensen, the sole surviving officer of that rank from World War 1.

Hitler did not speak at the opera house, leaving the address to his minister of defense, General Werner von Blomberg. Blomberg's words were chosen to reflect Germany's new confidence: "The world has been made to realize that Germany did not die of its defeat in the World War. Germany will again take the place she deserves among other nations." After the gathering in the opera house, Hitler, accompanied by his senior generals, walked down Unter den Linden, the broad, tree-lined boulevard that ran through central Berlin, to the Berliner Schloss, the old imperial palace. There he pinned crosses to the flags of the army. He and a huge, ecstatic crowd then watched a parade by units of the new army, which was overflown by aircraft from the air force.

Both the French and British, who had recently announced the build-up of their own armed forces, were alarmed by the turn of events. The British government attempted to persuade Hitler to join a Europe-wide mutual assistance pact. On March 25 Sir John Simon, the foreign secretary, and Anthony Eden, Keeper of the Privy Seal, paid a visit to Hitler in Berlin. Hitler was charm-

ing but blunt; he would not consider any pact that included the Soviet Union, claiming that German rearmament was a means to prevent the spread of communism in Europe. He rebuffed questions about his rearmament plans: "Did Wellington, when Blücher came to his assistance at Waterloo, first ask the legal experts of the Foreign Office whether the strength of the Prussian forces exceeded the limits fixed by treaty?"

On the second day of the meeting, Hitler responded to a question about the German air force's strength with a calculated bluff, declaring it the equal of Britain's. Both Simon and Eden were stunned, realizing that Hitler's demands were backed by substantial military power. Hitler, accompanied by Hermann Göring, prime minister and head of the Luftwaffe, and Joachim von Ribbentrop, the foreign minister, traveled to the British embassy in Berlin for a breakfast engagement. The ambassador, Sir Eric Phipps, had organized his children to give the Nazi salute as the guests arrived.

Although Hitler was much concerned with international diplomacy in the spring of 1935, he also fulfilled a number of social and political engagements. He had a key social event to attend on April 9. Göring married his second wife, the actress Emmy Sonnemann, at Berlin's town hall. Hitler played the role of witness to the proceedings. On May 1, National Labor Day, Hitler gave a speech at Tempelhof in Berlin to a crowd of

*Above:* **Berliners gather to cheer Hitler celebrating the return to the Third Reich of the Saarland in January 1935.**

*Right:* **Hitler's 1935 cabinet. The photograph was taken following the decision to reintroduce universal military service. From the left: Reichs Minister Dr. Hans Frank, Reichs Propaganda Minister Dr. Josef Goebbels, Otto Meissner, Reichs Interior Minister Dr. Wilhelm Frick, Minister Johannes Popitz, Minister of Education Bernard Rust, Prime Minister Hermann Göring, Reichs Minister of Justice Hans Kerrl, Reichs Foreign Minister Constantin von Neurath, Reichs Chancellor Adolf Hitler, State Secretary Dr. Hans Lammers, Reichs Defense Minister Werner von Blomberg, Reichs Economic Minister Dr. Hjalmar Schacht, Minister of Justice Dr. Franz Gürtner, Economics Minister Lutz Graf Schwerin von Krosigk, Reichs Minister Richard-Walther Darré, Reichs Minister of Transport von Eltz-Rühenach, Reichs Employment Minister Franz Seldte, Secretary of State Walter Funk.**

*Above:* **The memorial service for the Polish Marshal Josef Pilsudski in Hedwigs Cathedral, Berlin on May 18, 1935. Hitler arrives at the church for the service accompanied by Secretary of State Otto Meissner, his adjutant Julius Schaub, and driver Erich Kempka.**

*Right:* **Diplomats leave the Ministry of Justice on Berlin's Wilhelmstrasse after attending the 1935 New Year's reception.**

German workers. According to American journalist William L. Shirer, he appeared depressed with little of consequence to say.

On the evening of May 21 Hitler addressed the 600 or so members of the Reichstag in Berlin, claiming that his policies had been misunderstood and spoke of his belief in the pointlessness of war. "The blood shed on the European continent in the course of the last 300 years bears no proportion to the natural results of the events. If these states had applied merely a fraction of their sacrifices to wiser purposes, the success would certainly have been greater and more permanent." The carefully prepared speech, as much for foreign as domestic consumption, was a smokescreen. Earlier in the day Hitler had issued secret orders that made Dr. Hjalmar Schacht, the minister of economics, responsible for the economic preparations for war. Hitler also ordered the reorganization of the German Armed Forces (the *Reichswehr* became the *Wehrmacht*) with himself as its supreme commander. The Minster of Defense, Blomberg, became the Minster of War and Commander-in-Chief of the German Armed Forces.

The May 21 speech had a major impact in Britain, which had been moving toward agreeing a treaty on naval strengths with Germany. Early in June von Ribbentrop flew to London to secure the British government's signature to the treaty. The Germans agreed to limit their naval strength to 35 percent of

*Above:* **The civil wedding ceremony of Hermann Göring and the actress Emmy Sonnemann was held in Berlin Town Hall on 10 April 1935. Adolf Hitler acted as their witness.**

*Right:* **Closing parade by VIth Army Corps following exercises on the Luneburg Plain, September 2-7, 1935. From the left: Hitler, von Blomberg, von Fritsch.**

Hitler, von Blomberg, Chief of the General Staff Ludwig Beck (back to camera) and Field Marshal Fedor von Bock (at right) discuss a summer 1935 transport exercise at Grafenwöhr.

that of Britain, but were permitted to achieve parity with the Royal Navy in submarines. By acting alone, without its allies, chiefly France and Italy, Britain destroyed all hope of these powers presenting a united front against Hitler.

Hitler expressed his delight in recent events during the annual Nuremberg Rally in September. On the 16th he boasted of the army's role in Germany: "It is the army that has made men of us all, and when we looked upon the army our faith in the future of our people was always reinforced. This old glorious army is not dead; it only slept, and now it has arisen again in you." The day before, Hitler had addressed the Reichstag, which had been specially convened in Nuremberg. He demanded the passing of new laws, known as the Nuremberg Laws, that would severely restrict the rights of Germany's Jewish community. Henceforth German Jews would be denied citizenship, would be forbidden to marry ethnic Germans, and would be prevented from employing ethnic German servants. The Reichstag agreed to the measures.

One more opportunity was presented to Hitler in 1935 to prevent other European powers from presenting a united front against him. On October 3 the Italian dictator Benito Mussolini ordered his armed forces to invade Abyssinia. The attack was condemned by Britain, which demanded that sanctions be imposed on Italy. It was a move destined to infuriate Mussolini

*Right:* **Dr. Goebbels (holding the binoculars) and Himmler look on as Hitler delivers another party day rally speech.**

*Below:* **Hitler and Dr. Goebbels arrive to open Europe's largest building, the *Deutschlandhalle* in Berlin, on November 29, 1935.**

and push him closer to Hitler. The year ended with Hitler in a stronger position that ever. The strength of his armed forces was growing rapidly and the leading European nations who might have opposed his ambitions were falling out among themselves. Hitler would, in 1936, push forward his plans for the territorial expansion of Germany and forge closer ties with Fascist Italy.

# NUREMBERG RALLIES

Nuremberg

*Above:* **Nuremberg was chosen as the location for the Nazi Rallies because of its long history: that it was central, in Bavaria, and not too far away from Munich, the Nazis' spiritual home, were also strong points in its favor.**

*Above left:* **The Nazi party rallies—called *Parteitage* (Party Days) from 1926—started in January 1923 at Munich. The second was at Nuremberg in August 1923; the third at Weimar in July 1926. The 1927 rally was the fourth and the biggest to date. This photograph is from the 1927 Rally as Hitler greets members of the SA.**

*Left:* **Hitler at the fourth *Parteitag* to be held at Nuremberg on August 4, 1929. Alongside guests and party leaders he takes the salute on Nuremberg market square at the final march past.**

*Above right:* **Hitler views the plans for a Nuremberg Rally; he is accompanied by his adjutant Julius Schaub (right), Martin Bormann (left), and Max Amann (third from right)—the publisher of *Mein Kampf* and his literary agent.**

*Right:* **Adolf Hitler views the building site on the rally ground in Nuremberg. From the left is SS adjutant Günsche, Hitler's valet Wilhelm Krause, Mayor Liebel, Hitler, and the architect Albert Speer.**

*Above:* The rally of 1934 lasted for a week and was recorded for posterity by film director Leni Riefenstahl in the film *Triumph of the Will*. Here she and Heinrich Himmler discuss arrangements in the Leitpold Arena on September 9, 1934.

*Left:* Parade of the *Reichsarbeitdienst* (State Labor Service) at Nuremberg. They stand before the podium, stripped to the waist and holding shovels. At the front is Constantin Hierl, a leading SA figure, and Hitler.

*Right:* Hitler addresses 100,000 at the 1935 rally where he presented the Nuremberg laws on citizenship and race.

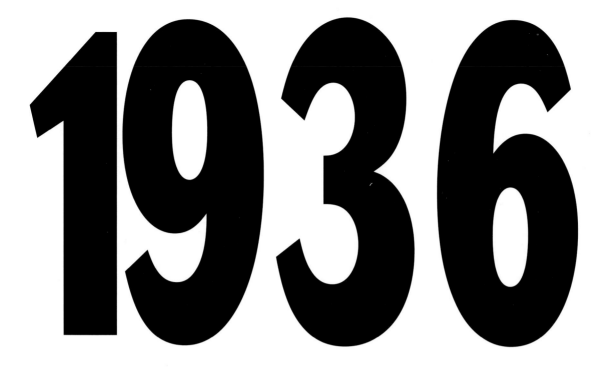

# 1936

Hitler began 1936 with one of the year's many propaganda coups; Germany staged the Winter Olympics in Garmisch in the Bavarian Alps during February. Hitler attended the events, which were choreographed to present the Nazi Party and Germany in the best possible light. It was a run-through for the Summer Olympics to be held in Berlin. While Hitler was keen to impress the world's press with spectaculars like the Garmisch games, he was also willing to take direct action to stake his claim as a powerful leader of a new, confident Germany. Although clearly nervous about the possible international response to any direct action, he decided to test the waters again, as he had done with the reoccupation of the Saarland in 1935.

Hitler's decision to embark on the diplomatic brinkmanship that would see regained the demilitarized Rhineland, an area that Germany had been forced to give up after World War 1, was prompted by the signing of a treaty between France and the Soviet Union in late February. Plans to reoccupy the Rhineland had been made the previous year, but senior generals were wary of implementing it because of the weakness of Germany's armed forces. However, despite this view, German troops reoccupied the Rhineland on March 7.

During the afternoon of the 7th Hitler appeared before the Reichstag in Berlin to explain his actions. Still worried about

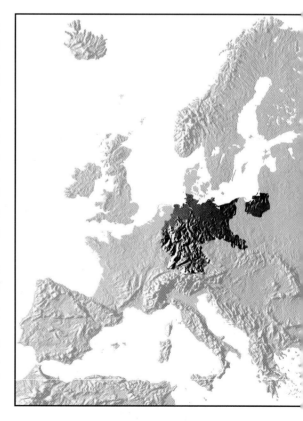

*Above:* **The boundaries of Germany at the end of 1936 during which year the Rhineland was reoccupied.**

*Above:* **On January 28, 1936 Hitler leaves the St George's Church, Berlin, after the memorial service for King George V of England who had died on January 20.**

*Below:* **Hitler views a model showing the rebuilding of the town of Kassel displayed in the town hall, accompanied by Adjutant Julius Schaub and Martin Bormann.**

possible responses to the events of the morning, he was in a conciliatory mood: "The German people have no interest in seeing the French people suffer. And what advantage can come to France when Germany is in misery?" The Reichstag's deputies rose to give Hitler a standing ovation, and other European powers failed to take any concerted action against Hitler's first diplomatic adventure of the year. Hitler also decided to seek a popular mandate for his action, calling for an election on the 29th.

Hitler traveled to the Rhineland shortly after its reoccupation and gave a speech at Cologne cathedral. During his return journey by special train, he expressed his relief that the other European powers had done little to prevent the operation: "Am I glad? Good Lord, am I glad it's gone so smoothly. Sure enough, the world belongs to the brave man. He's the one God helps. One can serve God only in the garb of the hero."

The prevailing sense in Europe was one of change, a feeling that the political realities created by the World War 1 peace treaties were about to undergo some deep-seated changes. Hitler himself caught the mood of the day during a speech at Breslau on March 22, just a week before election day: "We and all nations have a sense that we have come to the turning point of the age. Not only we, the former defeated, but the victors

also have the inner conviction that some think is wrong. Those who think that the word 'Versailles' could possibly stand at the entrance to a new order are sadly mistaken. That would not be the cornerstone of the new order, but its gravestone." A week after the Breslau speech, the Nazi Party won close to 99 percent of the votes cast.

The Spanish Civil War, fought between the Republican government and Nationalist forces under General Francisco Franco, began on July 17. The Soviet Union began to supply weapons to the Republicans, while Italy and, to a lesser degree, Germany sent military aid and personnel to Franco Nationalists. Hitler made the final decision to become involved in the war during a visit to Bayreuth. A German businessman, a local Nazi official, and a Spanish officer approached Hitler as he was returning to his temporary home after a performance at the city's opera house, the *Festspielhaus*, on July 25. They had with them a letter from Franco. Hitler agreed to Franco's request and sent a directive to Göring and Minister of War Field Marshal Werner von Blomberg. Hitler had made the decision to send financial and material aid, as well as the Condor Legion, to Spain.

The most prestigious event of 1936 was undoubtedly the Summer Olympics held in Berlin. It was a time for the Nazis to prove their international respectability and their strength. Nothing was left to chance as foreign guests had to be impressed. Attacks on Jews and Jewish property were greatly reduced under Nazi orders. On the first day of the games, Hitler was in attendance. The opening ceremony was watched by a crowd of over 100,000 and marked by a parade of 40,000 stormtroopers and a choir of 3,000, which sang the German national anthem and the *Horst Wessel Lied*. After the opening events, Hitler presented gold medals to the German winners of the shot and javelin events. The Olympic Committee complained that Hitler was only presenting to German winners, and he presented no more medals. To the Nazis' chagrin, the great athlete of the games was African-American Jesse Owens, who won four gold medals.

Hitler did return to the Olympic stadium for the closing ceremony on August 16, which was again stage-managed to the advantage of the Nazi Party. To complete the international

*Right:* Remembrance Day, Kassel, March 16, 1936. From the left: Walter von Brauchitsch, Admiral Erich Raeder, Wilhelm Reinhard (retired general and president of the Kyffhaus Society), Hitler, and Karl Weinrich, who was Gauleiter of Hesse-Kassel.

propaganda triumph, renowned film-maker Leni Riefenstahl produced a documentary of the games entitled *Olympia*, which was released in two parts: *Fest der Völker* (Festival of the Nations) and *Fest der Schönheit* (Festival of Beauty).

The Olympic Games were followed, in September, by the annual Nuremberg Rally. Again, no expense was spared to make the series of set-pieces a spectacular success. Each day was marked by huge events, each reflecting a particular aspect of Nazi Germany. Hitler gave a major speech on the 9th during which he announced a four-year plan to make Germany self-sufficient in raw materials. Together with the August announcement that conscription in Germany had been extended to two years, the Nuremberg four-year plan suggested that the rearmament and militarization of Germany was to be Hitler's top priority.

In the final months of the year, Hitler was, however, still preoccupied with forging closer ties with Italian dictator Benito Mussolini. On October 24, the Italian foreign minister, Count Galeazzo Ciano, paid a visit to Berchtesgaden. Hitler was keen to impress Ciano with his desire for significant links between the two dictatorships. He argued that the two needed to forge a close alliance against other European powers and the Soviet Union. He made plain that he considered Britain a potential

*Below:* **Berlin Olympic Games' opening ceremony, August 8, 1936.**

threat, against which both countries need to be prepared: "German and Italian rearmament is proceeding much more rapidly than rearmament in Great Britain. In three years Germany will be ready, in four years more than ready; if five years are given, better still."

Ciano had, in fact, already signed an agreement binding Italy and Germany together before meeting Hitler. Mussolini referred to it during a speech in Milan on November 1 in which he mentioned "an axis round which all those European states which are animated by a desire for collaboration and peace may work together." Japan was also linked to Germany in November with

*Above:* **In March 1936 Hitler was up for "re-election" and this photograph shows him at the beginning of an electioneering speech. It was, of course, all stage-managed. By this time all opposition parties had been banned and there could only be one outcome to any election.**

*Right:* **Adolf Hitler and Generaloberst Hans von Seeckt during an autumn exercise, September 26, 1936. Seeckt was hated by the Nazis because his wife was Jewish and he had organized the defeat of the Munich Beer Hall Putsch. He only avoided death in the 1934 purge by accepting the position of military advisor to China's Chiang Kai-Shek.**

*Left:* **Pictured together on the Day of German Art, November 12, 1936, Werner von Blomberg, Constantin von Neurath, and Adolf Hitler.**

*Below:* **At noon on December 30, 1936 Generaloberst Hans von Seeckt was carried to his grave with the highest military honors in the presence of an impressive line-up of Third Reich dignitaries. Pictured during the solemn burial, from left to right: General Gerd von Rundstedt, Admiral Erich Raeder, Generaloberst Baron Werner von Fritsch, Hitler, Generaloberst Hermann Göring, Field Marshal von Blomberg and Generaloberst von Heye (retired, far right).**

the signing of the Anti-Comintern Pact, an alliance created to combat the spread of the Soviet Union's influence.

Hitler was eager to present his recent diplomatic maneuvers as key to the survival of Europe's political freedom. At a speech in Munich on November 9, he stated that Nazi Germany was at the heart of the anti-communist alliance: "Perhaps the time is coming more quickly than we think when the rest of Europe will see in our Germany the strongest safeguard of a truly European, a truly human, culture and civilization. Perhaps the time is coming more quickly than we think when the rest of Europe will no longer regard with resentment the founding of a National Socialist German Reich, but will rejoice that this dam was raised against the Bolshevik flood."

At the end of the year, Hitler had cause to be pleased with the progress of his plans. Nazi Germany had been presented as a strong state capable of operating on the international stage. The Olympic Games had been prestigious affairs, designed for foreign consumption, while his takeover of the Rhineland had been a risky but successful coup. Alliances with Italy and Japan had strengthened his hand, particularly in Europe. He had transformed himself into a major international statesman and, with the rearmament program underway, he would have the military might to back up his diplomatic actions during 1937.

# HITLER'S ORATORY

Hitler was a spellbinding orator as was evinced strikingly at the Beer Hall Putsch Trial on February 24, 1924, when his speeches thrust him and his party into the limelight. His speeches were full of gestures and arm movements as this series of photographs show.

# 1937

Hitler determined to continue during 1937 the policies of building up Germany's strength that he had pursued in 1936. The rearmament program was progressing well and Hitler had growing confidence in his diplomatic maneuvers. In his speech on January 30, on the fourth anniversary of his chancellorship, Hitler spoke at length to the Reichstag. His prepared text covered many areas but he argued that Germany should have returned the colonies confiscated from it at the end of World War 1.

As the speech continued, Hitler made it plain that he also had territorial ambitions much closer to home. He mentioned, probably referring to the ethnic Germans living in the Sudetenland region of Czechoslovakia among others, "the justified feeling of national honor existing among those nationalities who are forced to live as a minority within other nations." Finally, he remarked that Germany, although not looking for confrontation, had the means to back up its demands: "We move through the world as a peace-loving angel, but one armed in iron and steel."

This was a theme he returned to the next month. On the occasion of the anniversary of the Nazi Party's founding, February 24, Hitler addressed an audience in Munich. Gloating on his recent diplomatic successes with Italy and Japan, he was able to announce that: "we have once again become a world power." As in confirmation of Germany's growing military power,

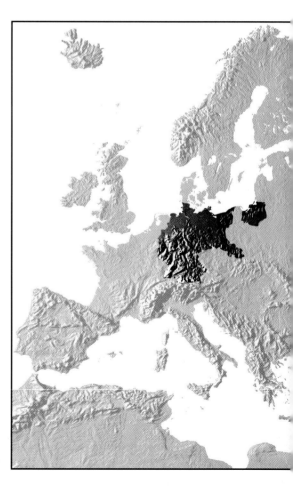

*Right:* **31 sailors were killed on the pocket battleship *Deutschland* when the ship was bombed by Spanish Republican aircraft off Ibiza on May 29. The men were buried at Wilhemshaven in the presence of Hitler and Minister of Defense, Field Marshal Werner von Blomberg.**

*Below:* **Hitler greeted by enthusiastic crowds as he arrives at the State Operette Theater in Munich—the town of German Art—on November 21, 1937 for the opening performance. The theater on the Gartnerplatz had been extensively rebuilt on Hitler's orders and was festively decorated for the opening performance of *Die Fledermaus*.**

*Below left:* **Germany's boundaries at the end of 1937.**

Hitler's birthday celebrations in Berlin on April 20 included a major parade, which he watched from the city's Technical College.

Hitler was determined to make advances on the diplomatic front. On May 4 he met Lord Lothian, hoping to persuade the British official that a united bulwark against communist expansion would be of benefit to both countries. Hitler stated that he was at a loss to understand why Britain, a country he had always admired, refused to recognize the dangers, and added that a second war between Germany and Britain would be disastrous to both. Lothian report back to London and there the matter rested for six months. Evidence of Germany's military commitment in Spain came later in the month when the German warship *Deutschland* was attacked by Spanish Republican aircraft on the 29th. Around 20 crewmen were killed and Hitler later traveled to the port of Wilhelmshaven to attend their funeral, which was conducted with full military honors.

Whatever the immediate difficulties Hitler was encountering on the diplomatic front, he was much more confident and convinced of the role he had been destined for. Speaking in Würzburg on June 27, he put it bluntly: "I am well aware of what a man can do and where his limits lie, but I hold to the conviction that men who have been created by God ought also live in accordance with the will of the Almighty. God did not create the races of this Earth in order for them to give themselves up, to bastardize and ruin themselves."

By the time of the annual Nuremberg Rally, Hitler again aired his views on the conspiracy between communists and Jews. On the 13th, in his closing speech, he argued that German troops were fighting in the Spanish Civil War to prevent the spread of the "Jewish-Bolshevik conspiracy" and that he was at a loss to understand why neither the French or British would aid him in the National Socialist "crusade" against the threat. Hitler was still casting around for firm allies and again turned to Mussolini.

During the same month Mussolini paid a state visit to Germany. Hitler was particularly concerned over Italy's agreement with Britain—signed on January 2—that affirmed that the current balance of power in the Mediterranean should remain. Various senior Nazis, including Göring, Foreign Minister Joachim von Ribbentrop, and Minister of War Field Marshal Werner von Blomberg among others, had been sent to Rome on diplomatic missions throughout the year. Mussolini set out for Germany on September 23, first meeting Hitler in Munich, where the Italian dictator was impressed by a military parade. After visits to the army training grounds at Mecklenburg and the Krupp industrial complex at Essen, Mussolini arrived in Berlin by special train, where Hitler was waiting to greet him again.

Berlin was decked out to impress Mussolini. Architect and designer Benno von Arent had created a triumphal avenue along Berlin's Unter den Linden. Mussolini and Hitler attended a mass rally in the Maifeld, adjacent to the 1936 Olympic Stadium. A crowd of over 750,000 had been gathered to see the two dictators. Hitler praised Mussolini, saying that he was: "One of those lonely men of the ages on who history is not tested, but who themselves are the makers of history." However, Mussolini was left to make his own way from the ceremony, becoming drenched due to a heavy downpour. Hitler was clearly in the dominant position. And, despite the fiasco at the Maifeld, Mussolini returned to Italy hugely impressed by Hitler and Nazi Germany.

Hitler, although well satisfied with the impression left on Mussolini by the September state visit, was still a man in a hurry to push forward his plans. He was acutely concerned that he might not be strong enough to complete them and that there would be no one of suitable stature to continue his work. Addressing a gathering of propaganda officials in October, he explained that only he could be relied on to complete the task in hand. As one of those present recorded: "It is therefore necessary to solve the problems that had to be solved [German territorial expansion] as quickly as possible so that this could still be done in his lifetime. Later generations would no longer be able to do it. Only he himself was still in a position to."

*Above:* **The car carrying Mussolini and Hitler arrives at the Krupp factory in Essen, the town known as the "Armorer of the German Reich," on September 27, 1937.**

*Right:* **Lord Halifax, the British Foreign Secretary, and to the left the British Ambassador Sir Nevile Henderson with Göring on his country estate November 20, 1937.**

November saw a flurry of diplomatic activity that seemed to confirm that Hitler's confidence in Germany's new-found strength and power was not misplaced. On the 5th Hitler played host to the Polish ambassador, Lipski, in Berlin's Reichs Chancellery. Hitler was able to secure an agreement regarding the fate of Danzig, a free-port with a large German ethnic presence, but separated from Germany by the so-called "Polish Corridor" at the end of World War 1. Hitler stated that there would be no alteration to the status of Danzig and that Germany had considerable interest in keeping Poland strong as a guarantee against any attempts by the Soviet Union to expand its influence westward.

The same day, however, Hitler addressed a small gathering of senior officers and Nazi politicians in the Reichs Chancellery. Among those present were Göring, Blomberg, General Werner von Fritsch, the commander-in-chief of the army, Admiral Erich Raeder, commander of the navy, and Constantin von Neurath, a senior diplomat. Minutes taken by a colonel, Hossbach, showed that Hitler was contemplating war: "Germany's problem could only be resolved by means of force, and this was never without attendant risk."

In Rome a day later, the 6th, Ribbentrop secured Mussolini's signature to the Anti-Comintern Pact, an agreement that greatly angered the British. The British response was to send Lord Halifax, the representative of the new prime minister, Neville Chamberlain, to Germany later the same month. Halifax first traveled to Berlin to visit a hunting exhibition at Göring's request. Halifax then went to Berchtesgaden, where he met Hitler. Hitler argued that Britain could still not accept that Germany was no longer a weak power and that Britain was unwilling to enter into discussions regarding Germany's territorial claims. When Halifax reported back to Chamberlain, he stated that he believed that the key questions raised by Hitler during their discussions on the 19th related to the future of Danzig, Austria, and Czechoslovakia.

At a speech in Augsburg on November 21 in front of his old comrades from the early days of the party, Hitler returned to the themes that he had spoken on during his speech on January 30. The tone was ominous: "What the world shuts its ears to today, it will not be able to ignore in a year's time. What it will not listen to now, it will have to think about in three years' time, and in five or six years' time, it will have to take into practical consideration." His passage continued: "I am convinced that the most difficult part of the preparatory work has already been achieved. Today, we are faced with new tasks, for the *Lebensraum* (living space) of our people is too narrow." These were ominous words as the events of 1938 were to prove.

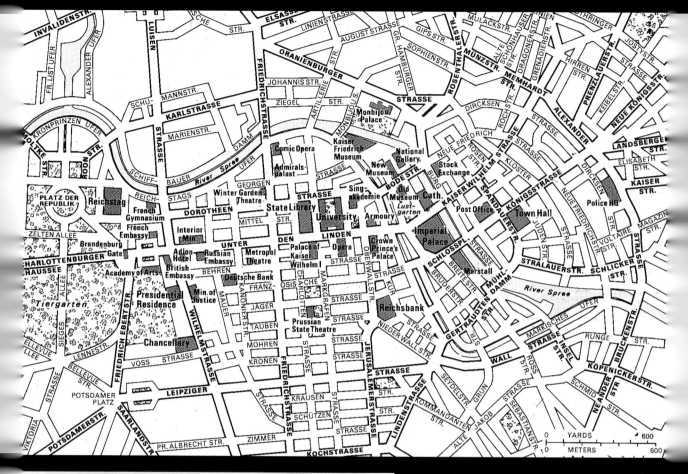

*Above:* **Berlin of the 1930s.**

*Left:* Unter den Linden is one of the grandest thoroughfares in Berlin and the main east-west axis, ar on it was the memorial to the German fallen in Wo War I at which the annual remembrance ceremonie were held. The memorial was a neoclassical buildir designed by Karl Friedrich Schinkel in the 19th cenry as a police station and called the Neue Wache ( page 42). It was converted into a memorial for the military dead of World War 1 in 1930-31. Here President Paul von Hindenburg is pictured with his son, Oskar, and Hitler during the February 25, 1934 ceremony.

*Above right:* Driving past troops lined up on parade procession of cars travels west down the then Charlottenburgerstrasse (with the Brandenburg Ga in the background) on August 25, 1938. Admiral vc Horthy, the regent of Hungary, is in the car with Hi

*Right:* Accompanied by Sepp Dietrich and Rudolph Hess on his right and Heinrich Himmler to his left, Hitler salutes a parade by the Leibstandarte-SS Ad Hitler, his personal bodyguard, along Wilhelmstrass on January 30, 1938—the fifth anniversary of the d he became chancellor.

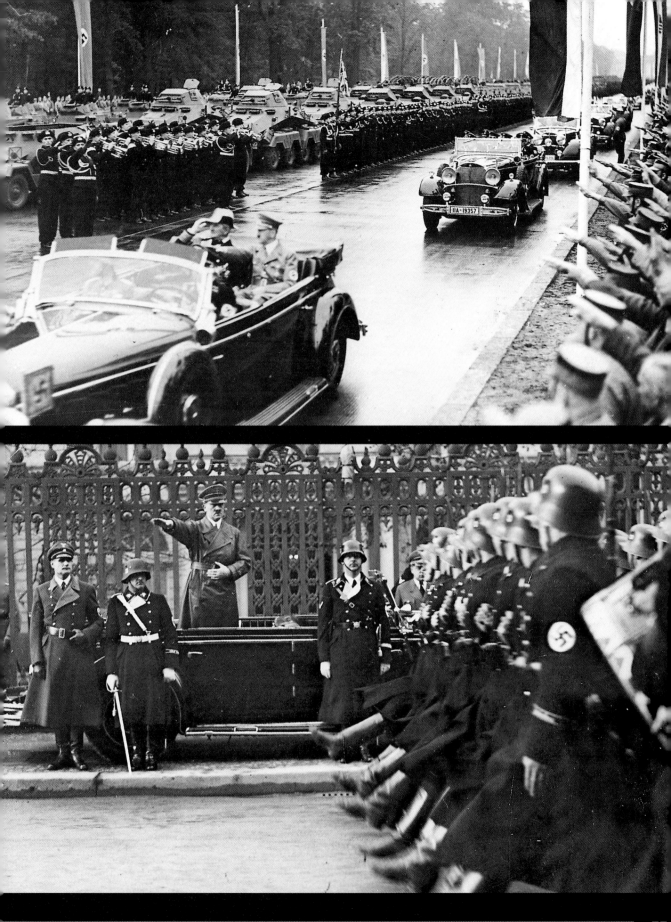

*Left:* Another review of the Leibstandarte; this one is on February 20, 1938.

*Below left:* Taken around 1930 before it was burned, to the left of this photograph of the centre of Berlin is the Reichstag Building. The Brandenburg Gate is on the right.

*Bottom left:* Imperial Palace (viewed from the water side) and cathedral before the war.

*Right:* Hitler saluting his birthday parade by the Leibstandarte-SS Adolf Hitler in Wilhelmstrasse, on April 20 1938, from outside the Presidential Palace.

*Below right:* January 30, 1938: Hitler stands on the balcony of the Reichs Chancellery surrounded by a crowd of 10,000, in the flag-bedecked Wilhelmstrasse on the anniversary of accepting the German chancellorship in 1933.

*Below far right:* German Panzer I tanks parade before Hitler at the Brandenburg Gate, before heading down the Charlottenburgerstrasse.

# 1938

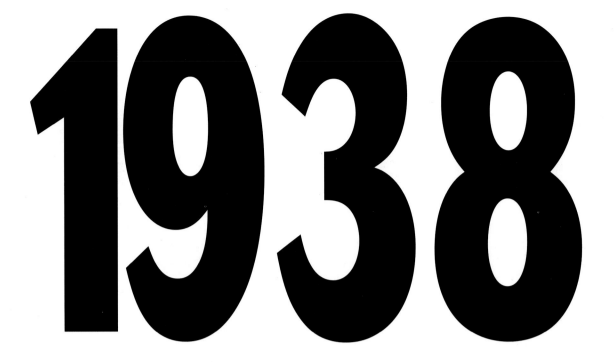

At the beginning of 1938 Hitler moved swiftly to consolidate his hold on Germany's armed forces by removing key members of the old conservative establishment. First to go was Minister of War and Commander-in-Chief of the Armed Forces Field Marshal Werner von Blomberg. On January 12, Blomberg married an actress, Eva Gruhn. Both Hitler and Hermann Göring witnessed the ceremony. It was then revealed that Gruhn had been a prostitute and posed for pornographic pictures. Senior officers met Hitler and argued that Blomberg had disgraced the army and embarrassed them all. Blomberg was sacked, but the obvious replacement, General Werner von Fritsch, Blomberg's commander-in-chief of the army, was not acceptable to many leading Nazis.

On January 26 Fritsch was summoned to a midday meeting at the Reichs Chancellery in Berlin. Hitler confronted him with documents—provided by Heinrich Himmler, head of the Gestapo secret police, and Göring—that detailed a series of homosexual liaisons and also had on hand a young man, Hans Schmidt, who identified Fritsch as one of his blackmail targets. Schmidt's story was bogus, concocted under secret police pressure, and Fritsch maintained a dignified silence. No immediate decision as to Fritsch's fate was made and the quarrel continued over the following days. On February 4 Hitler met his cabinet, explaining that Blomberg had been relieved of his

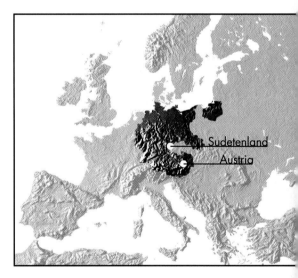

*Above:* **Germany's boundaries at the end of 1938.**

*Top right:* **Hitler speaks to a huge crowd from the platform in front of Vienna's Hofburg on March 15, 1938, shortly after** *Anschluss*—**the take over of Austria.**

*Right:* **Hitler and the Italian king, Victor Emmanuel III, in Rome on May 8, 1938. The state visit to Italy took place shortly after the** *Anschluss.* **The night before Hitler had attended a state banquet in the Palazzo Venezia.**

duties and that Fritsch had surrendered his post on the grounds of his poor health. Hitler, already supreme commander of the armed forces, abolished the post of minister of war. At a stroke, Hitler had taken complete charge of Germany's military machine.

The following day at Berchtesgaden Hitler asked to see Franz von Papen, former deputy chancellor and the German ambassador to Austria since 1934. Hitler ordered Papen to organize a meeting with Dr. Kurt von Schuschnigg, the Austrian federal chancellor. Austrian Nazis had been agitating for German to take over Austria. Schuschnigg, accompanied by Austrian Secretary of State for Foreign Affairs Guido Schmidt, traveled north from Salzburg by car late on February 11 to get Hitler's confirmation that he had no intention of becoming involved in Austrian affairs.

The two men were met by Papen at the frontier and they motored together up to the Berghof, where Hitler was waiting to greet them on the steps on the morning of the 14th. Talks began in Hitler's study. He said: "I can tell you, here and now, Herr Schuschnigg, that I am absolutely determined to make an end of all this. The German Reich is one of the Great Powers, and nobody will raise his voice if it settles its border problems. I can only wait until this afternoon. If I tell you that, you will do well to take my words literally. I don't believe in bluffing."

In the afternoon Schuschnigg was confronted with Hitler's demands: the ban on the Nazi Party in Austria was to be lifted; leading Nazis were to be appointed to the government, including Arthur Seyss-Inquart as minister of the interior; the Austrian economy was to be integrated into that of Germany's; and that the two countries' armies were to be closely linked. Hitler stated: "You [Schuschnigg] will either sign as it is and fulfil my demands in three days, or I will march into Austria." The document was signed.

Schuschnigg, however, had one last card to play. He decided that Austrians should vote on the issue of *Anschluss* (union) with Germany. News of his plan reached Hitler in Berlin on March 9 and he immediately summoned Göring and General Wilhelm Keitel, the chief of staff of the high command of the German armed forces, to the Reichs Chancellery. Plans for the invasion of Austria were quickly drawn up, but were to be implemented only "if other measures proved unsuccessful." In the early morning of March 11, German troops began moving toward the Austrian border. Later in the day, amid growing scenes of confusion in Austrian government circles and unrest on the streets, Seyss-Inquart was ordered to prepare to form a government from a list of names decided upon by Berlin.

By midday on the 12th Hitler and Keitel were at the field headquarters of the German Eighth Army and a little later Hitler crossed over the border with Austria and made his way to Linz, where he had once studied. There he was met by Seyss-Inquart and General Edmund Glaise-Horstenau, a pro-Nazi Austrian minister. Hitler addressed the waiting crowds: "If Providence once called me forth from this town to be the leader of the Reich, it must, in so doing, have charged me with a mission, and that mission could be only to restore my dear homeland to the German Reich." Hitler stayed in Linz overnight, visiting his parents' grave at Leonding on the 13th and then, back in Linz later that evening, received news that the Austrian government had accepted his demands.

Hitler entered Vienna in triumph on the 14th. Crowds thronged the city center to salute him, yet he stayed just one night, returning to Berlin the next day. Hitler addressed the Reichstag on the 18th and told the assembled deputies that the Reichstag was to be dissolved and that new national elections, including Austria, were to be held on April 10. He asked that the Nazi Party be granted another four years of power. Hitler hit the campaign trail with a vengeance. In the first week or so of April, he visited Austria, stopping off at Graz, Klagenfurt, Innsbruck, Salzburg, and Linz. The whirlwind electioneering culminated in a mass rally in Vienna on the 9th. The vote on the 10th was a forgone conclusion; the Nazis took over 99 percent of the votes. Hitler talked of his joy during a press conference: "For me this is the proudest hour of my life."

At the beginning of May, Hitler, still basking in his successful take over of Austria, headed for Rome on a state visit. Four

*Left:* **A Jewish synagogue in flames. During the** *Kristallnacht* **(Crystal Night) pogrom of November 9-10, 1938, 74 Jews were killed and 20,000 arrested. Jewish homes and businesses were attacked and nearly 200 synagogues destroyed. The attacks were ordered by Reinhard Heydrich, chief of the SD, in retaliation for the assassination of Ernst von Rath, Third Secretary of the German Embassy in Paris, by a Polish Jew.**

*Below:* **Hitler at Munich railway station on his return from his state visit to Italy, May 10, 1938.**

special trains were needed to transport Hitler and other leading Nazis, including Foreign Minister Joachim von Ribbentrop, to Italy for the meeting with Benito Mussolini. Hitler spoke of his admiration for the great beauty of Florence and Rome, but was most eager to patch up his relations with the Italian dictator, who had not been wholly happy with the take over of Austria as it threatened Italy's interests in the South Tyrol. On May 7, there was a state banquet at Rome's Palazzo Venezia. Hitler's speech strove to reassure his host: "It is my unalterable will and my bequest to the German people that it shall regard the frontier of the Alps, raised by nature between us both, as for ever inviolable." In private, Hitler informed Mussolini that he intended to take over Czechoslovakia.

Hitler returned to Germany, where on May 20 he was informed by Keitel that the German forces stationed on the Czech border could advance with just 12 hours' notice. More worryingly, Hitler was also informed that the Czechs had mobilized their own powerful armed forces. A hasty council of war was convened at the Berghof on the 22nd. Hitler was not ready for war with Czechoslovakia, and was worried by the possible responses of Britain, France, and Poland, so ordered the situation to be defused. Hitler's apparent climb down was seized upon by the foreign press and Hitler spent a week at the Berghof raging against their reports.

On May 28 Hitler flew back to Berlin and arranged a meeting with senior Nazis in the Reichs Chancellery. Among those present were Göring, senior cabinet member Constantin von Neurath, and Ribbentrop. Four top generals were also in attendance: Keitel, General Ludwig von Beck, the chief of the general staff, General Walter von Brauchitsch, the army's commander-in-chief, and Admiral Erich Raeder, head of the German navy. Hitler outlined his plans for Operation "Green," the onslaught against the Czechs.

Over the next three months Hitler launched a diplomatic offensive to pave the way for the attack on Czechoslovakia. Britain and France played into his hands, suggesting that the Czech government look favorably on the demands of those ethnic Germans living in the country's Sudetenland region to unite with Germany. The Poles were seen as being eager to gain part of Czechoslovakia. Hungary, although willing to see Czechoslovakia carved up, needed more persuading. At a meeting in Kiel in late August Hitler held talks with the Hungarian regent, Miklos Horthy, and senior government ministers. The Hungarians remained lukewarm, and Hitler was heard to remark that "he who wanted to sit at table must at least help in the kitchen." Military preparations for Operation "Green" continued, however.

Hitler's generals were, nevertheless, concerned that the attack on Czechoslovakia, would provoke a Europe-wide war. Hitler ordered a meeting at the Berghof on August 10. He deliberately excluded many of the older generation of generals and appealed directly to those of a lesser age. He spoke for three hours, outlining his plans and reassuring them. Toward the end of the meeting Hitler invited a discussion; some of those present doubted the wisdom of the venture. Hitler exploded at their lack of conviction. Beck resigned his post as chief of the general staff over the argument. Despite the frank exchange of views, Hitler continued to advance the plans for Operation "Green." On September 3 he met Keitel and Brauchitsch at the Berghof. Hitler made it plain that units earmarked to carry out the attack had to be ready by September 28.

Hitler traveled to Nuremberg for the annual rally between September 6 and 12. He again met with Keitel, Brauchitsch, and General Franz Halder, the new chief of staff, on the 9th. During a late night-early morning meeting, he raged against the slow progress being made for the implementation of Operation "Green." However, the start date for the attack was put back to the 27th. On the final evening of the Nuremberg Rally, Hitler hinted at his willingness to go to the aid of the Sudeten Germans in Czechoslovakia: "The Germans in Czechoslovakia are neither defenseless nor are they deserted, and people should take notice of that."

The final day at Nuremberg was also marked by an uprising by ethnic Germans in the Sudetenland. The rebellion was put down by the Czechs and several thousand Nazi supporters, including their leader Konrad Henlein, fled to Germany. Events in Czechoslovakia in the middle of September so alarmed the British that their prime minister, Neville Chamberlain, flew out to meet Hitler to discuss matters. The meeting took place at the Berghof in the middle of the afternoon of September 15. Hitler and Chamberlain, accompanied by only Hitler's interpreter, Paul Schmidt, held their talks in the first-floor study. Hitler lectured Chamberlain for some time and then, much to the prime minister's growing anger, made his position plain: "I am determined to settle it [the Sudeten issue]; I do not care whether there is a world war or not. I am determined to settle it and settle it soon; I am prepared to risk a world war rather than allow this to drag on."

Chamberlain left the Berghof the following day and Hitler subsequently returned to Berlin. On the 20th he met senior Hungarian ministers to urge them to reiterate their territorial claims against the Czechs. The pressure on the Czechs was intensified two days later when Henlein led a body of Sudeten Germans back into Czechoslovakia and took over the towns of Eger and Asch. Chamberlain intervened once again, flying to a

*Left:* **Adolf Hitler on the Schöber Line after the occupation of the Sudetenland.**

*Below left:* **Hitler speaking at the Nuremberg Rally of September 6-12, 1938: it would prove to be the last of the Nazis' great showpieces, involving a million people. Next September the parading would be for different reasons.**

*Below:* **The Munich conference, September 29-30, 1938. On the far right Hitler looks thoughtful as he discusses the situation with his generals. From the left: Wilhelm Keitel Chief of Staff of the Army High Command covering his mouth, Quartermaster-General Karl Heinrich von Stülpnagel (later hanged for his involvement in June 1944 bomb plot), and speaking, General Johannes von Blaskowitz (later to command the invasion of Poland).**

meeting with Hitler at Godesberg near Bonn on the River Rhine on the same day.

At Godesberg, Hitler stayed in the Hotel Dreesen, from where he had organized the Blood Purge of 1934. Chamberlain stayed in the Hotel Petersberg on the other side of the Rhine. The meetings, which began in the afternoon, took place in the Hotel Dreesen. Chamberlain had in fact secured the Czech government's agreement to giving up the Sudetenland, but for Hitler the plan was far too late. He stated: "I'm exceedingly sorry but after the events of the last few days this solution is no longer any use." The next day Chamberlain tried, but failed, to get Hitler's agreement to a compromise over the Sudetenland. At the final evening discussion on the 23rd, Hitler demanded that the Czechs complete their withdrawal from the Sudetenland by the 28th, and then as a concession changed the date to October 1. Chamberlain believed he had a little breathing space to find a solution.

Hitler returned to Berlin after the meeting. On the 28th, a few hours before he was to give a speech at the Sportpalast, he met Sir Horace Wilson and the British ambassador, who had the results of Chamberlain's most recent talks with the Czechs. They were rejected out of hand. Hitler screamed: "There's no point at all in going on with negotiations. On October 1 I shall

have Czechoslovakia where I want her." Addressing the crowd at the Sportpalast later, Hitler made clear his plans: "Before us now stands the last problem that must be solved and will be solved. It is the last territorial claim which I have to make in Europe, but it is the claim from which I will not recede and which, god willing, I will make good."

The following day, just two days before Hitler's ultimatum ran out, Berlin saw a flurry of diplomatic activity. The first to visit Hitler in the Reichs Chancellery was the French ambassador, André François-Poncet, who stated that Hitler's plans for the phased occupation of Czechoslovakia between October 1 and 10 were acceptable. (The Czechs had not been informed of this.) The Italian ambassador, Bernardo Attolico, arrived while Hitler was still in discussion with François-Poncet. Mussolini, alarmed at the possibility of an all-out European war, had decided to intercede on Britain's behalf. Hitler met briefly with Attolico and agreed to delay making any decision on France's proposals for 24 hours. The final visitor was Britain's Sir Nevile Henderson, the British ambassador, arrived to suggest a international conference to discuss Czechoslovakia. Hitler agreed and requests to attend were sent out to London, Paris, and Rome—but not Prague or Moscow.

Hitler decided to meet Mussolini before the conference, so on the following day, September 29, he climbed on board the dictator's personal train at Kufstein at what had been the border between Germany and Austria. Hitler explained to Mussolini his plans to invade Czechoslovakia first and then France. Mussolini did, however, persuade Hitler to give the forthcoming international conference a chance. The conference began the same day at the new *Führerhaus* in Munich. Because the meeting had been arranged so urgently, it had little structure, although it began with Hitler reiterating his demands

The British delegation was headed by Chamberlain and included Henderson, Douglas Dunglass, later Prime Minister Douglas Home. The French premier, Edouard Daladier, attended with his foreign minister, Alexis Leger, and François-Poncet. Mussolini was accompanied by Count Galeazzo Ciano, his foreign minister. Hitler's entourage included, among others, Göring, Himmler, Keitel, Ribbentrop, and Hitler's deputy, Rudolf Hess. The series of meetings were concluded in the early hours of the 30th; Hitler was allowed to take over the Sudetenland. His troops marched into the former Czech region on October 1. Munich had been a brilliant coup by Hitler.

Hitler had taken over the Sudetenland without going to war, but he remained adamant that foreign powers should refrain from, as he saw it, interfering in German affairs. At a speech in Saarbrücken on October 9 Hitler said: "Inquiries of British politicians concerning the fate of Germans within the frontiers of the

*Right:* **The Munich Conference, September 29-30, 1938. From the left: British Prime Minister Neville Chamberlain, French Premier Edouard Daladier, Adolf Hitler, the Italian leader Benito Mussolini and the Italian Foreign Minister Count Galeazzo Ciano.**

*Below:* **Hitler is welcomed into the Sudetenland at Wildenau.**

Reich—or of others belonging to the Reich—are not in place. We would like to give these gentlemen the advice that they should busy themselves with their own affairs and leave us in peace." There were still over 250,000 ethnic Germans in what remained of Czechoslovakia. Hitler gave similar speeches at Weimar on November 6 and then again at Munich two days later.

During the middle of October Hitler invited François-Poncet to Obersalzberg. The French ambassador was entertained not, as was usual, in the Berghof but at the Hitler's personal home, the Eagle's Nest, which lay some 6,000ft (1,830m) up a mountain and was reached by a 10-mile (16km) twisting mountain road. Hitler did not hide his dissatisfaction with the settlement at Munich and British diplomacy, but also made the suggestion that France and Germany sign a joint declaration confirming their mutual border. The French agreed. Hitler also sought to strengthen his ties with Italy. Later in the month, Ribbentrop traveled to Rome to suggest a formal pact between Germany, Italy, and Japan.

The year ended with Hitler in a strong position. He had greatly expanded the Third Reich's territories, greatly increased the strength of its armed forces, and driven a wedge between those European powers who might oppose him. Over the next 12 months, he would use his newly-won strength to launch further political and military adventures that would lead to the outbreak of World War 2.

# DIPLOMATIC MEETINGS

*Top left:* Hitler greets Pierre Laval, Premier of Vichy
France, the main agent of Nazi power in France. This was possibly in Munich in November 1942, following Allied landings in North Africa. It was at this time that Laval was told that the Germans would occupy Vichy France. Laval had already raised a French Nazi army, allowed Frenchmen to be deported as forced labor to Germany, and turned a blind eye to Nazi atrocities in his own country.

*Below:* In early June 1939 Prince Paul of Yugoslavia made a state visit to Berlin. He is seen here with Adolf Hitler, Minister Johannes Popitz and Herman Göring. Their collective aim was to keep Poland isolated.

*Right:* Admiral Miklos von Horthy on his arrival in Berlin joins Hitler to review navy and air force companies in front of the railway station at Lehrter. Horthy, an Hungarian patriot, would try his best to keep Hungary out of World War 2, but sided with Germany rather than Russia.

*Below right:* On the last day of his Berlin visit, August 25, 1938, the Hungarian Regent, Admiral Miklos Horthy, and his wife attended a farewell reception hosted by the Foreign Minister Baron Joachim von Ribbentrop. Hitler escorts Frau von Horthy as they arrive for the reception. To the right is Wilhelm Frick, and Town President Dr. Lippert, in the background next to von Ribbentrop is the admiral, who is escorting Frau von Ribbentrop.

*Above left:* **Hitler with Arthur Seyss-Inquart, the pro-Nazi Austrian Minister of the Interior; following the *Anschluss* he became the head of *Ostmark* (the Nazi name for Austria). This picture was probably taken in March 1938 after the *Anschluss*.**

*Above:* **One of the key diplomatic meetings of the 1930s took place at Munich on September 29, 1938. It was primarily concerned with the Sudetenland crisis. Pictured in the *Führerhaus* or Munich's Königsplatz are from the left: Benito Mussolini, Hitler, Edouard Daladier (shaking hands), and Dr. Paul Schmidt, Hitler's chief interpreter.**

*Left:* **Hitler and Philippe Pétain, who ran Vichy France for the Nazis—he said he did it to save the French from subjugation.**

*Above right:* **The meeting of Hitler and Chamberlain at Munich's *Führerhaus*, September 29-30, 1938. From the left: Joachim von Ribbentrop, Neville Chamberlain, Hitler.**

*Right:* **Architectural exhibition, Munich, December 10, 1938. From the left: Heinrich Hoffmann, Hitler's photographer; Dr Robert Ley, the leader of the Nazi Labor Front; Bernardo Attolico, the Italian ambassador to Germany; an interpreter; Hitler, and the architects.**

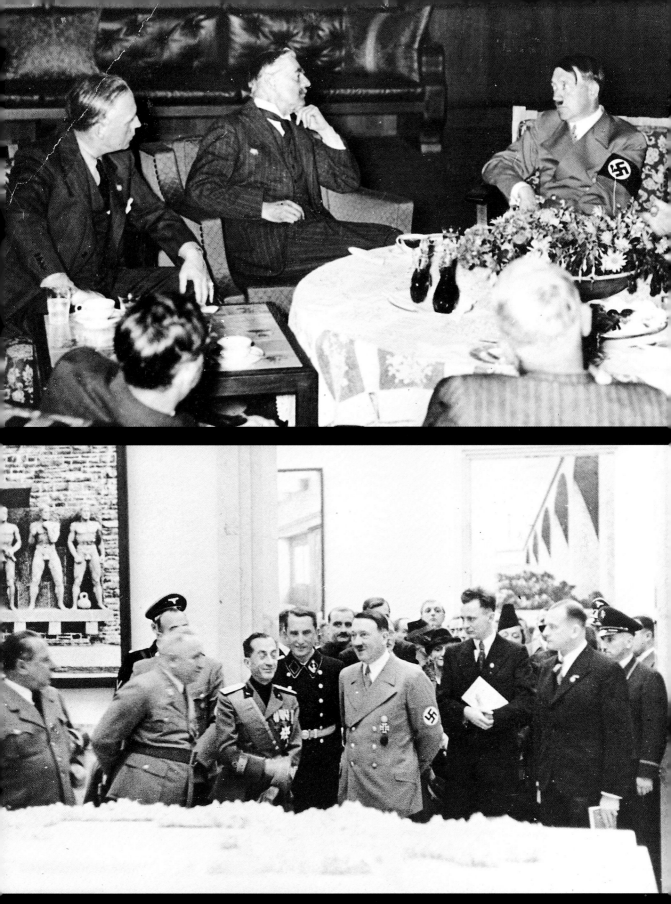

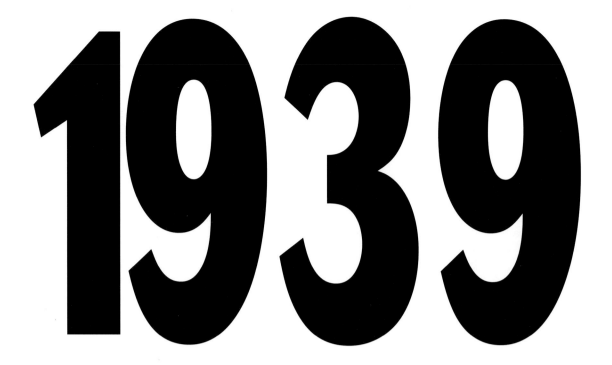

# 1939

In the first day of 1939 Hitler continued to make it plain that Germany had no ambitions toward Poland. He met Colonel Josef Beck, the Polish foreign minister, at Berchtesgaden in January. At a meeting between the two on the 5th, Hitler made it clear, however, that he wanted to reincorporate Danzig into the Third Reich: "Danzig is German, will always remain German, and will sooner or later become part of Germany." Beck rejected the return of Danzig to Germany outright. Hitler did not seemingly press the matter. However, Hitler continued his program to strengthen Germany's armed forces but in January had to deal with opposition to his policy from the president of the Reichsbank, Dr. Hjalmar Schacht. Schacht met Hitler in Berlin on January 7 and was dismissed from his post. Schacht was replaced by Walther Funk and the bank was placed under Hitler's direct control.

Hitler had already made up his mind to take over what remained of Czechoslovakia, and met the Czech foreign minister, Frantisek Chvalkovsky, in Berlin in January. Hitler was not looking for compromise but issued a list of demands that he knew would be unacceptable to the Czechs. Hitler wanted to add Czechoslovakia's arms industry to Germany's and make use of the country's economy for the benefit of the Third Reich. Hitler decided to exploit the nationalist aspiration of the Slovakians, who were eager to break away from the Czech

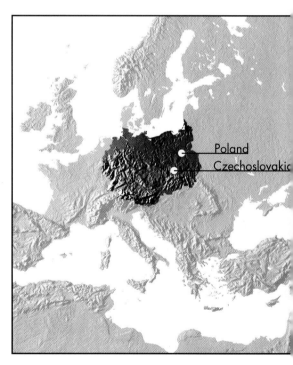

*Above:* **The boundaries of Germany and conquered territories at the end of 1939.**

*Right:* **Celebration of the founding of the party in the *Hofbräuhaus* in Munich, February 24, 1939. Accompanying Hitler are Rudolf Hess and Martin Bormann.**

state. He met Dr. Bela Tuka, leader of the Slovak National Party, and Franz Karmasin, head of the ethnic German minority in Slovakia, in the Reichs Chancellery on February 12. Tuka fell in step with Hitler's plans, stating: "I lay the destiny of my people in your hands, my Führer; my people await their complete liberation from you."

However, the Slovaks did little to further the break up of Czechoslovakia, particularly after the Czech authorities imposed martial law in Slovakia, and Hitler was forced to apply further pressure. He had talks with Catholic priest Josef Tiso, the head of the Slovakian government, and Ferdinand Durcansky, another member of the government. The meeting took place in the Reichs Chancellery during the early evening of March 13. Hitler forcefully expressed his disappointment at the Slovaks' lack of action. And made thinly veiled threats. Tiso returned to Bratislava, where he read a statement prepared by the Germans that announced the break-away of Slovakia.

The Czechoslovakian president, Emil Hacha, and Chvalkovsky traveled by train to Berlin to seek out a compromise immediately after the Slovak announcement. Their visit had all the trappings of a state visit, but Hacha's meeting with Hitler in the Reichs Chancellery was to the point. Hitler made it

*Above:* **Adolf Hitler and Dr Emil Hacha, President of Czechoslovakia, meet in Berlin in March or April 1934. Hacha was made president when Czechoslovakia became a protectorate of the Third Reich and ceased to be a sovereign state from November 1938. He was yet another Nazi puppet ruler and only nominally in charge of his country.**

plain that the German armed forces would invade Czechoslovakia later that day (March 14) and that to avoid bloodshed and the destruction of Prague, Hacha should sign a document inviting the Germans to occupy Czechoslovakia. Hacha, a tired, frightened old man, agreed.

Hitler traveled to Prague on the 15th accompanied by Foreign Minister Joachim von Ribbentrop, Heinrich Himmler, head of the SS, and Wilhelm Keitel, chief of the general staff. Hitler and his entourage spent the night in the palace of the king of Bohemia and the next day, from Prague's Hradschin Castle, announced that Germany had territorial claims on the provinces of Bohemia and Moravia. Hitler then published a decree announcing the creation of the Protectorate of Bohemia and Moravia, in effect, a puppet state. Hitler did not stay long in Czechoslovakia. He watched a triumphal march by German troops in the capital, paid a flying visit to Brunn, and was in Vienna by the 18th.

Hitler now turned his attentions to Memel, a strip of land along the northern border of East Prussia that Germany had given up to Lithuania as part of the Versailles settlement. Lithuania was far too weak to oppose the Third Reich, and a week after Hitler had been reviewing his troops in Prague, he arrived in Memel by boat. Hitler spoke to the Germans there on the 23rd: "You have returned to a mighty new Germany, a

*Above left:* **Dr. Neumann, the leader of the local party, greets Hitler at the celebration for the reunification of Memel with the German Reich on March 22, 1939. From the left: Martin Bormann, Adolf Hitler, Karl Wolff (Himmler's liaison officer to Hitler), Luftwaffe General Karl-Heinrich Bodenschatz (Göring's liaison officer with the High Command of the Wehrmacht) and Dr. Neumann.**

*Above:* **June 6, 1939, saw a parade and ceremonies for the Condor Legion: those who fought in Spain. Here in the Berlin Lustgarten, Hitler speaks from a platform in front of the city's neoclassical Altes Museum.**

Below: **Prince Regent Paul of Yugoslavia and his wife with Hitler on their state visit to Berlin, June 7, 1939.**

Germany determined to be the mistress of her own destiny and herself to fashion that destiny, even if that should not please the world without. For this new Germany today over 80 million Germans take their stand."

Alarmed by Hitler's growing pressure on Poland, the British prime minister, Neville Chamberlain, announced on March 31 that Britain would go to Poland's aid if Poland was threatened by military action. The French government also made a similar commitment. Hitler, speaking at Wilhelmshaven on April 1, made it clear that he would not be intimidated: "If anyone should really wish to pit his strength against ours with violence, then the German people are in the position to accept the challenge at any time." On April 3 Hitler ordered his generals to prepare for three military scenarios: the defence of Germany's frontiers, an attack on Poland, and the take-over of Danzig. Operation "White," the invasion of Poland, was to begin on September 1. Hitler knew that war with Poland would certainly mean war with Britain. At a meeting with the Romanian foreign minister, Gregoire Gafencu, in the Reichs Chancellery on April 19, Hitler seemed unworried by the prospect: "Well, if England wants war, she can have it."

Hitler spent little time in Berlin between the end of April and the beginning of August, preferring to stay in Berchtesgaden. There were, however, a number of state visits to Berlin by various leaders of other European states with whom Hitler wanted to curry favor to isolate Poland further. The Hungarian prime minister and foreign minister arrived at the end of April to be followed by the regent of Yugoslavia, Prince Paul, who arrived in early July. Hitler set out to impress the Yugoslavian regent, who attended the Berlin opera, a state banquet, and watched a military parade; and at the beginning of July, the Bulgarian prime minister visited Berlin.

However, Hitler was most eager to forge closer ties with Italian dictator Benito Mussolini. After weeks of careful negotiations the "Pact of Steel" between the two was signed in Berlin on May 22. Hitler looked on in the Reichs Chancellery as Ribbentrop and Ciano, signed the treaty documents. The Axis was established. Italy's fortunes were now inextricable bound up with those of the Third Reich.

The following day, Hitler met his senior generals from all three services in his study in the Reichs Chancellery. He made it clear that Poland was to be attacked, irrespective of whether or not Britain and France would intercede: "We must burn our boats. It is no longer a question of right or wrong, but of life or death for 80 million human beings." Hitler, however, needed to prevent any military alliance between Britain, France, and Russia before he could invade Poland. Negotiations between the Soviet Union and Germany had been underway since early

May, but as the weeks passed with no obvious signs of progress, Hitler became more impatient.

By the beginning of August, the situation in Danzig was deteriorating. On August 7 the German *Gauleiter* (political head) of Danzig visited Hitler at Obersalzberg, where it was made plain that Hitler's patience was wearing thin. Four days later, Carl Burckhardt, the League of Nations commissioner responsible for Danzig, paid Hitler a visit at Obersalzberg. Hitler threatened the Poles in their talks as Burckhardt noted: "If the slightest thing was attempted by the Poles, he [Hitler] would fall upon them like lightning with all the powerful arms at his disposal." Ciano, visiting Berchtesgaden on the 12th and 13th, was left in no doubt about Germany's war plans. His diary entry records that "after the conquest of Poland Germany would be in a position to assemble for a general conflict 100 division on the West Wall [the border fortifications with France]."

While Hitler remained at Berchtesgaden in late August, the treaty with the Soviet Union, the Non-Aggression Pact, was close to completion. It was signed by Ribbentrop in Moscow on the 24th, by which time Hitler had flown back to Berlin. On the 25th Hitler met the British ambassador, Sir Nevile Henderson, followed by the Italian ambassador, Bernardo Attolico, and later his French counterpart, Robert Coulondre. None of the

*Below left:* **Stalin with Hitler's Foreign Minister, Joachim von Ribbentrop, together in Moscow for the signing of the Russo-German treaty on August 24, 1939.**

*Right:* **Adolf Hitler visits Danzig on September 22, 1938. From the left: press chief Dr. Otto Dietrich, Albert Bormann, Hans Junge, Köster, Dr. Karl Brandt (one of Hitler's doctors), Schaub, Hitler, Martin Bormann, Bodenschatz, and Karl Wilhelm Krause, Hitler's valet.**

*Below right:* **Adolf Hitler visiting the front in Poland, 1939. Behind him is Martin Bormann. Fourth from the right: SS Gruppenführer Karl Wolff, Himmler's liaison officer to Hitler.**

conversations went Hitler's way and he was forced to reconsider the timetable for the invasion of Poland. The next day, however, he regained his nerve and confirmed the invasion for September 1.

Despite a last-minute flurry of diplomatic activity in the final days of August, German forces unleashed their Blitzkrieg against Poland precisely on schedule. Hitler addressed the Reichstag at the Kroll Opera House during the morning of September 1 and concluded with these ominous words: "I have once more put on that [soldier's] coat that was the most sacred and dear to me. I will not take it off again until victory is secured, or I will not survive the outcome." On September 3, Britain declared war on Germany

The attack on Poland went spectacularly well. Hitler made his headquarters at Gogolin in a specially converted train, but then traveled towards the rapidly advancing front line. On the 18th he set up his headquarters at the Casino Hotel in the Baltic town of Zoppot, and on the following day made his entry into Danzig. Hitler returned to Germany at the end of September by which time the Polish armed forces were virtually destroyed. Hitler could now begin planning for the invasion of France and the Low Countries.

However, conservative elements in the armed forces were opposed to Hitler's wish to continue the war and plotted his assassination. Finally, on November 8 they had their chance. Hitler traveled to Munich, where was to attend the annual gathering of old Nazi Party members at the city's Bürgerbräukeller. Hitler, however, cut short his speech, and so left before the bomb had exploded. He was given the news of the assassination attempt as he made his way back to Berlin by train. He stated: "Now I am content! The fact that I left the Bürgerbräukeller earlier than usual is a corroboration of Providence's intention to allow me to reach my goal." The war would continue in 1940.

*Left:* **Hitler with the List Regiment—16th Bavarian Infantry Regiment—at Christmas 1939. This was the unit with which Hitler served in World War 1, as, coincidentally, did Rudolf Hess for a time, but they did not meet until much later.**

*Left:* Hitler spent a great deal of time at Berchtesgaden, a Bavarian town some 75 miles southeast of Munich. Here he would use slave labor to build his hideaway, the "Eagle's Nest," and cultivate the image of the caring, friendly people's leader.

*Below:* The "Eagle's Nest" some 2,000m higher than the Berghof, and reached by an 120m elevator journey.

*Right:* Reviewing the construction site of the small tea house at the Berghof. From the left: Adolf Hitler, his adjutant Wilhelm Brückner, Martin Bormann, press chief Dr. Otto Dietrich, and Dr. Karl Brandt, one of Hitler's doctors, Reichs Commissioner for Health and head of the euthanasia program.

*Below right:* Hitler greets young visitors in front of the steps to the Berghof, accompanied by his adjutant Wilhelm Brückner.

*Above:* Women from the Braunau region—the small Austrian village where Hitler was born—visit Hitler at the Berghof to pledge their devotion, making for a good photo opportunity.

*Right:* Hitler plays with his dogs while out walking at the Berghof. Hitler was a noted dog-lover and vegetarian.

*Right:* **To foster the image of a kindly man, Hitler was photographed feeding deer on the terrace at the Berghof.**

*Below:* **Hitler's Berchtesgaden chalet, the SS barracks in the grounds of the house, and his mountain refuge at the top of the Obersalzburg, were attacked on the morning of April 25, 1945 by Lancasters of RAF Bomber Command, escorted by Mustangs of the US 8th Air Force and RAF Fighter Command. 12,000lb "Tallboy" bombs fused for deep penetration were used. The picture shows the barracks, left-centre, partially obscured by smoke during the attack. In the lower central foreground is Hitler's chalet. The picture was issued in 1945.**

# 1940

By the beginning of 1940, there were attempts to bring an end to the hostilities in Europe. Hitler, however, laid plans to extend the war by first invading Denmark and Norway, and then, with his northern flank secure, by launching a Blitzkrieg against France and the Low Countries. Hitler began the year by addressing the German people, readying them for the fighting that was to follow. However, his public speaking engagements in 1940 were, in fact, few—just seven in the year. In private, he focused on bolstering his alliance with the Italian dictator, Benito Mussolini.

On January 30, at a time when plans for the invasion of Denmark and Norway were being put in train, Hitler appeared at Berlin's Sportspalast on the seventh anniversary of his coming to power. His speech poured scorn on the attempts of other European powers to diffuse the growing tension. Hitler stated that, "The apostles of international understanding cannot once again betray the German nation." Some three weeks later, on February 24, Hitler spoke in Munich, preparing the German people for war and attempting to justify the turn of events. His text ended with a reminder of Germany's fate in World War 1: "If in those days a certain Adolf Hitler had been chancellor of the German Reich instead of a musketeer in the German Army, do you believe that the capitalist idols of international democracy would have won?"

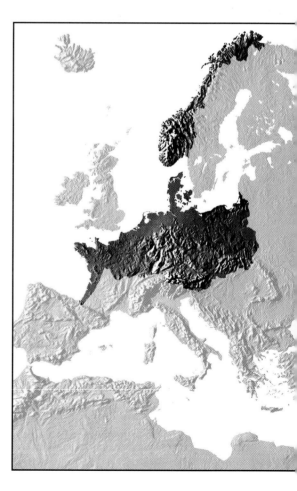

*Above:* **Munich, June 18, 1940. Hitler is received at the main railway station by the *Alte Kämpfer* after the successful Western Campaign and just before his meeting with Italian Foreign Minister, Count Galeazzo Ciano, and Mussolini. To the right stands Ritter von Epp, the former leader of the *Freikorps* and Hitler's governor of Bavaria, and Martin Bormann.**

*Below left:* **The boundaries of Germany and the land seized by the Nazis at the end of 1940.**

*Below:* **Heroes' Remembrance Day at the Berlin Arsenal, March 16, 1940.**

While Hitler was preparing the German people for war, he was also pushing ahead with preparations for the takeover of Denmark and Norway, and engaging in frantic diplomacy. Hitler met the man chosen to lead the descent on Norway, General Nikolaus Falkenhorst, in Berlin on February 20. After a short conference, Falkenhorst was ordered to prepare rough plans for the assault and return with them at five o'clock when Hitler approved Falkenhorst's hastily written outline. On March 2, Hitler met the U.S. Undersecretary of State Sumner Welles in the Reichs Chancellery. Welles was there to broker some form of peace settlement before full-scale war broke out, but he left the meeting without making any progress. Hitler made clear his aims: "at the very worst, all will be annihilated."

Hitler, although set on war, still harbored concerns about Italy's support for his aims. He despatched his foreign minister, Joachim von Ribbentrop, to Rome for talks with his Italian counterpart, Count Galeazzo Ciano, on March 10. The Italian leader, Benito Mussolini, agreed to support Germany in a war, but did not offer any specifics, so Hitler proposed that the two of them should hold talks at the Brenner Pass on March 18. Hitler handled Mussolini well, talking over his recent triumphs in Poland and the preparations for the campaign in Western Europe. As Ciano recorded, Mussolini was won over: "The Duce repeated

that, as soon as Germany has by her military operations created a favorable situation, he would lose no time in intervening." Hitler did not mention the forthcoming attacks on Denmark and Norway, however. These were launched on April 9 and, despite Anglo-French landings in Norway, had reached a successful conclusion by late May, although by then the campaign had been overshadowed by events in France and the Low Countries.

On May 10, the day that Operation "Yellow"—the attack on France—began, Hitler moved to his forward headquarters, the *Felsennest* (Cliff Nest), at Bad Münstereifel, some 30 miles (48km) from the Belgian frontier in the heart of the Black Forest. The Blitzkrieg attack went extraordinarily well, but Hitler remained worried by the magnitude of the undertaking. His chief of the general staff, General Franz Halder, wrote on May 17: "Führer is terribly nervous. Frightened by his own success, he is afraid to take any chance and so would rather pull the reins on us." Hitler's forces, however, were equal to the task and his armored divisions swept across northern France. By the end of May, the bulk of the French and British forces had been crushed, although the evacuation of some 338,000 troops from Dunkirk in late May and early June, soured the victory. Paris was occupied on June 14 and the French asked for an armistice on the 16th.

The Italians had somewhat belatedly joined the campaign against France on June 10, and Hitler agreed to meet Mussolini and Ciano in Munich on June 18. The meeting lasted two days. Mussolini wanted to cash in on Germany's victory by taking over France's North African colonies, but Hitler was lukewarm to the idea. He argued that France might balk at the idea and be prepared to resume hostilities rather than expect such humiliating conditions. Hitler, basking in the glory of his recent military successes, held all the trump cards in the argument and Mussolini backed down. Ciano reflected his and Mussolini's feeling toward Hitler at the meeting: "I cannot be said to hold especially tender feelings for him, but at this moment I really admire him."

Hitler departed Munich on July 20 and flew back to his field headquarters, the *Wolfsschlucht* (Wolf's Glen), near the Belgian village of Brûly-de-Pesche, where he and his staff worked on the final armistice terms. Hitler operated from the *Wolfsschlucht* between June 6 and 25, finally leaving when the swarms of gnats that hovered about the place became too much. Throughout the night, Paul Schmidt, Hitler's interpreter, and others worked by candlelight in the village church to produce a French-language version of the document. Hitler's choice of where the armistice would take place reflected his continuing resentment at Germany's humiliation in World War 1. He chose

the same location in the Forest of Compiègne, northeast of Paris, where France's Marshal Ferdinand Foch had dictated the surrender terms to Germany's representatives on November 11, 1918. To complete France's humiliation, the very same restaurant car that had been the scene of the 1918 meeting was hurried removed from a Parisian museum and set up on exactly the same spot it had occupied at Compiègne in 1918.

Hitler and his delegation arrived at Compiègne during the afternoon of the 21st. With Hitler were Hermann Göring, Joachin von Ribbentrop, Rudolph Hess, General Wilhelm Keitel, Admiral Erich Raeder, and the German Army's commander-in-chief, General Walter von Brauchitsch. The French representatives were Vice-Admiral LeLuc, General d'Aviation Bergeret, General Huntziger (who signed the armistice document the next day), and M. Léon Noël. Inside the carriage, Hitler occupied the chair used by Foch in 1918. He stayed briefly to hear the preamble to the surrender terms and then he and his entourage left to return to the *Wolfsschlucht*. Hitler walked to his waiting Mercedes as the band played the German national anthem and the *Horst Wessel Lied*. The non-negotiable details of the surrender document were read to the French by General Alfred Jodl (who would have the positions reversed on May 7, 1945 at Rheims when he would sign Germany's unconditional surrender to the Allies). Northern and eastern France were to be occupied; the south and west were to become a puppet state—Vichy.

Hitler now took the time to bask in his great triumph. On June 28 he flew to Paris accompanied by several art and architecture experts, including Albert Speer. The three-hour visit began at the Opéra and also took in the Champs-Elysées, the Eiffel tower, the tomb of the Emperor Napoleon at Les Invalides, the Place de la Concorde, and ended at Montmartre, which Hitler later described as "appalling." Hitler spent the remainder of the month touring the battlefields of World War 1 and traveled to Alsace. In the first week of July, He spent some time back at the *Felsennest*.

Hitler returned to Berlin in triumph, although plans for a celebratory parade were canceled for fear of Royal Air Force bombing raids, and met with Ciano on July 7. Ciano again

*Top left:* **Hitler and Mussolini in Munich during their two-day meeting, June 18-19, 1940.**

*Left:* **Parade after the Western Campaign, Berlin, July 18, 1940. Standing on the balcony of the Chancellery from left to right: Hitler, Göring, Günsche, and Bodenschatz.**

pressed Hitler to allow Italy to take over France's colonies, but Hitler reiterated that he had no wish to antagonize either the British or French. Although France had fallen, Hitler was eager to reach some accord with Britain and its Prime Minister Winston Churchill. However, it soon became clear that Churchill would not enter into negotiations. Hitler addressed the Reichstag at Berlin's Kroll Opera House on the 19th: "Mr. Churchill ought, perhaps for once, to believe me when I prophesy that a great [British] empire will be destroyed. I do, however, realize that this struggle, if it continues, can end only with the complete annihilation of one or the other of the two adversaries. Mr. Churchill may believe that this will be Germany. I know that it will be England." Three days before the Kroll Opera House speech, Hitler had issued Directive Number 16, the order to begin planning the invasion of England, codenamed Operation "Seelöwe" (Sea Lion).

Although preparations for Operation "Sea Lion" were underway, Hitler expressed concern over the undertaking. On July 21 he talked of his worries to Raeder at the Reichs Chancellery: "The invasion of Britain is an exceptionally daring undertaking— the crossing of a sea which is dominated by the enemy. If it is not certain that preparations can be completed by the beginning of September, other plans must be considered." Minutes of a meeting at the Berghof on July 31 indicated that Hitler would not contemplate an invasion without total air superiority over

*Left:* **Compiègne, June 21, 1940. From the left: von Brauchitsch, Raeder, Hitler, Hess, Göring, and von Ribbentrop. Behind them are Adjutants Schmündt and Brückner. Hitler, exultant after the defeat of France, delivered to French envoys the German terms of surrender. Compiègne was deliberately chosen as the same spot where Germany had been humiliated and forced to sign the armistice after World War 1 on November 11, 1918.**

*Below:* **Meeting between Hitler and Franco at the Spanish-French border in Hendaye, October 24, 1940.**

the English Channel. British victory in the Battle of Britain made sure that their would be no invasion in the summer of 1940. Operation "Sea Lion" was finally canceled on January 9, 1941, but by that time Hitler was completing his plans for an attack on the Soviet Union. The idea of attacking the Soviet Union had been first mooted in July and the momentum had built up during the second half of the year.

Hitler engaged in a flurry of diplomatic activity throughout the second half of 1940, most directed at Italy, Spain, the Soviet Union, and Vichy France. On September 17, Spain's foreign minister, Serrano Suner, was presented to Hitler at the Reichs Chancellery. Spanish dictator General Francisco Franco had offered somewhat conditional military support to Germany, but had cooled to the idea once it became clear that Britain would continue the war. Hitler tried to charm Suner into giving a definite commitment, but the foreign minister would not, although mightily impressed by the opulent chancellery and Hitler's poise. A second meeting, however, left him less impressed and Suner departed for Rome, leaving the matters in hand unresolved. Hitler remained unhappy over Spain's demands for allying with Germany. At a meeting in the chancellery with Ciano on the 28th, Hitler expressed doubts that "Spain had the same intention of will for giving as well as taking." Nevertheless Hitler decided to persevere with Spain over the following months. Hitler's diplomatic activities did bear some fruit on September 27, when Germany, Italy, and Japan agreed to sign the Tripartite Act in Berlin.

On October 4 Hitler held a meeting with Mussolini at the Brenner Pass. Mussolini was worried that Hitler was being too friendly toward Vichy France and that Spain was trying to take over some of France's North African colonies that "rightly" belonged to Italy. Hitler explained that he could not afford to antagonize Vichy France by surrendering its colonies to Spain as this might lead them to declare for the Free French government under General Charles de Gaulle in England. By implication this suggested that Hitler would also not let Italy take over France's North Africa colonies. Mussolini remained unhappy at the direction of Hitler's seemingly conciliatory foreign policy toward Vichy France was taking and later wrote to Hitler, saying that France, "who thought, because she had not fought, that she had not been beaten," was being treated far too leniently.

Hitler determined to continue his dialogue with Spain and France, and suggested face-to-face meetings with both Franco and Pétain. Hitler met Franco first, on October 23 at Hendaye in southwest France on the Franco-Spanish border. The meeting lasted nine hours. Hitler demanded that Spain should declare war on Britain in January 1941 and launch an immediate attack on the British base at Gibraltar. Franco requested that

German supply Spain with vast quantities of arms and fuel, and agree to Spain taking over France's North African colonies. The discussion went round in circles, neither side fully trusting the other, and no firm agreement was reached. Hitler later spoke of his frustration at Franco's intransigence, "rather than go through which again, I would prefer to have three or four teeth taken out."

Hitler's next meeting, on the following day, October 24, was with Pétain and his deputy, Pierre Laval. Pétain was a man Hitler professed to admire, but he found Laval "a dirty democratic politician, a man who doesn't believe in what he says." The talks were held at Montoire, and in return for Vichy France receiving some of Britain's African colonies, France would have to "bear the territorial and material costs of the conflict." Pétain may have believed that he had little choice other than to accept Hitler's proposal that his regime collaborate with Germany, but the details of the scheme were never hammered out. Pétain may have been playing a waiting game. His comments to a friend suggest that he was not willing to tie Vichy France's fortunes that closely to those of Germany: "It will take six months to discuss this programme and another six months to forget it." Nevertheless, history's view of Pétain is one of collaborator.

Hitler left the meeting with Pétain with perhaps the wrong impression. Immediately following his discussions at Montoire, Hitler traveled in his special train to Florence. He met Mussolini on the 28th and declared that the pact with Vichy France was "of great interest and help to the Axis, not so much from the military point of view as from the psychological effect it will have on the British when they see a compact continental bloc against England being formed." Mussolini and Hitler held their talks in the city's Pitti Palace. Hitler's sudden decision to travel to Italy was, in fact, not to discuss Franco or Pétain, but to deal with the potential crisis created by Mussolini's invasion of Greece from Albania, which had begun the same morning.

Hitler had not been informed of Mussolini's plans, which he considered dangerously destabilizing and directly opposed to his own geopolitical ambitions, but kept his rage in check. On the journey back to Germany, Hitler's interpreter, Paul Schmidt, summed up Hitler's mood: "He went north that afternoon with bitterness in his heart." Although he may not have fully realized the situation, Hitler's diplomatic efforts with Vichy France and Spain had effectively failed, and Mussolini's invasion of Greece were to have profound effects on the course of the war.

Mussolini's invasion did not go well and it became clear that German troops would have to be committed to the campaign. Hitler had been planning to invade the Soviet Union since the summer, but did not wish to attack until the build up of his forces along the Eastern Front had been completed.

*Above:* **The signing in Berlin of the Axis Pact between Germany, Italy, and Japan on September 27, 1940. At the table from the left: Kutusu, the Japanese Ambassador in Berlin; Count Ciano, Italian Foreign Minister; behind him German Interior Minister Otto Meissner, then Hitler, and von Ribbentrop (speaking).**

Below: **Molotov and Hitler met in Berlin in November 1940; they are shown with their interpreter Gustav Hilger. Vyacheslav Mikhailovich Molotov was Russian Foreign Minister 1939-49 and already well-known as Stalin's uncompromising advisor.**

Involvement in Greece and the Balkans would obviously delay the concentration of forces in the east and could possibly provoke Soviet military involvement in the Balkans. Hitler, in consultation with Foreign Minister Joachim von Ribbentrop, decided to mollify the Soviet leadership.

The Soviet foreign minister, Vyacheslav Molotov, arrived in Berlin on November 12 and met Hitler at the Reichs Chancellery. Hitler began by offering a high-flown overview of the situation. Molotov said nothing until Hitler had finished and then asked a series of pointed questions that caught Hitler unawares. Hitler broke off the meeting immediately, using the pretext of the danger of a possible air raid. The meeting broke up, but was reconvened the following day. Again harsh words and pointed questions were exchanged, but no satisfactory settlement was reached. Shortly after his last meeting with Molotov, Hitler saw Göring and made it clear that the invasion of the Soviet Union, Operation "Barbarossa," was to go ahead. Shortly after Molotov's departure from Berlin, Hitler ordered that a suitable site had to be found for permanent headquarters in the east—Rastenburg in East Prussia was chosen..

On November 20, the Italian Foreign Minister, Count Ciano, held talks with Hitler in Vienna, making it plain that he would help the Italians in the Balkans. German troops would be committed to the campaign there and help stabilize the badly mauled Italian forces in North Africa, which were crumbling under British attacks. Hitler believed that Yugoslavia was the key to the Balkans. To attack there, he needed the support, or at least the acquiescence, of several Balkan states. Meetings were held in November in Germany with King Boris of Bulgaria, the Romanian dictator General Ion Antonescu, and the Yugoslavian foreign minister, Cinkar-Marcovitch.

The year closed with Hitler determined to deal with the crisis in the Balkans through the use of military force, yet he still believed he could stick to the timetable for the invasion of the Soviet Union, scheduled to begin on May 15, 1941. He did, however, feel the need to reassure the German people. On December 10 at the Rheinmetall-Borsig armaments works in Berlin, he talked to workers and nurses of the social reforms to be introduced after the war, justified the war, and allayed their fears over British bombing raids on the capital: "If the British Air force drops two or three or four thousands kilograms of bombs, we will drop a hundred and fifty, a hundred and eighty, two hundred thousand kilograms, and more in a night. No matter what happens, England will be broken. That is the only timetable I have. And if today, in England, people are inquisitive and ask: 'But why doesn't he come?'—they may rest assured: he'll come all right." Hitler, of course, had already effectively abandoned his invasion plans for Britain.

Felsennest
Wolfsschlucht
Tannenberg

Adlerhorst
Wolfsschlucht 2

*Above:* **German paratroops and infantry pictured at a Dutch crossroads in May 1940.**

*Above right:* **In Hitler's headquarters—the** *Wolfsschlucht*—**in Belgium during the Western Campaign, in 1940. From the left: Ernst Udet, chief Aircraft Inspector-General, Schaub, Hitler, Göring, Bormann.**

*Right:* **Hitler's headquarters during the Western Campaign, 1940. Amongst others pictured are: to Hitler's right Field Marshal Wilhelm Keitel, the chief of staff; to his left Alfred Jodl, chief of operations; Karl Wolff, and Martin Bormann.**

*Left:* **The fall of the western powers in such a short space of time made a huge difference to the map of Europe.**

# 1941

Hitler made a keynote speech at Berlin's Sportpalast on January 30, 1941, outlining his hopes for the new year. He claimed that: "1941 will be the crucial year of a Great New Order in Europe. When the other world has been delivered from the Jews, Judaism will have ceased to play a part in Europe. Those nations who are still opposed to us will some day recognize the greater enemy within."

During the first few months of 1941, Hitler was chiefly preoccupied with two issues: the need to resolve the developing crisis in the Balkans and the need to push ahead with the plans for the invasion of the Soviet Union, despite it leading to Germany having to fight on two fronts in Europe.

On January 8-9 he met with the senior officers of the army, navy, and air force at the Berghof to discuss the situation in the Balkans, concluding that a large military force would be committed if needed. Ten days later, Mussolini, still smarting from recent defeats in North Africa and Greece, and Ciano arrived at the Berghof. The meeting lasted two days and Hitler spent two hours on the second day speaking on his planned attack on Greece. Mussolini was not informed of the attack on Russia.

Hitler went ahead with his plans to deal with Greece. For this he needed the compliance of various Balkan states. He met with Yugoslavia's Prince Regent Paul in early March, securing his agreement to allow German troops transit through his coun-

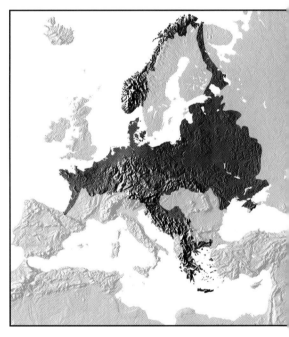

*Above:* **Germany's boundaries and conquered territories at the end of 1941.**

*Right:* **Heroes' Remembrance Day, March 16, 1941, at the Berlin Arsenal. Listening to Hitler are—first row from the right: Propaganda Minister Dr. Josef Goebbels, leader of the Labor Front Dr. Robert Ley, Minister of Education Bernard Rust, Heinrich Himmler, Hitler's deputy Rudolf Hess, Commander of the German Navy Erich Raeder, Army Commander-in-Chief Walter von Brauchitsch, Chief of Staff of the Armed Forces' High Command Wilhelm Keitel, Luftwaffe Director of Armaments Field Marshal Erhard Milch.**

*Above:* **Hitler spent April 30, 1941 in Marburg, Austria, on the Drau river, where he enjoyed an enthusiastic reception from the population. From the left: Bodenschatz, Hitler, Wolff, Überreiter, and press chief Dr. Otto Dietrich.**

try. This was confirmed in Vienna on March 25, when the Yugoslavian foreign minister, Dragisa Tsetkovitch, met with Hitler and his ministers to sign a pact. Hitler's plans were thwarted on the 26th, when a group of Yugoslavian officers opposed to the pact deposed the regime and installed a new king, Peter II. Hitler was furious and ordered the invasion of Yugoslavia. His decision, taken in haste, had profound implications. The invasion of Russia would have to be postponed while Yugoslavia was dealt with.

Hitler was also keen for Japan to enter the war against Britain at the earliest possible date, believing Britain would be thus placed under too much pressure to fight Germany and hold its possessions in the Far East. The Japanese foreign minister, Yosuka Matsuoka, had discussions with both Hitler and his foreign minister, Joachim von Ribbentrop, in the Reichs Chancellery at the end of March, immediately after the meeting to attack Yugoslavia had been concluded. Despite Hitler's request that Japan attack the British base at Singapore quickly, Matsuoka explained that Japan was not prepared to attack Singapore at the moment.

On March 30 Hitler called together 250 of his generals at the Reichs Chancellery in Berlin to allay their fears of a war on two fronts: "Now the possibility exists to strike Russia with our

rear safe. I would be committing a crime against the German people if I did not seize it." Hitler went on to explain the type of campaign that would be waged: "The fight will be very different from the fight in the west. In the east harshness is kindness toward the future. The leaders must demand of themselves the sacrifice of overcoming their scruples."

German forces invaded Yugoslavia and Greece on April 6 and operations were concluded successfully by the beginning of May. Hitler, fearing that Germany's victory would heap further humiliation on Mussolini, who had singularly failed to achieve very much in the Balkans, addressed the Reichstag in Berlin on May 4: "The concentration of German forces was therefore not made for the purpose of assisting the Italians in Greece. It was a precautionary measure against the British attempt to entrench themselves in the Balkans." The reality was that Germany's victory had confirmed that Italy was very much the junior partner in the Axis alliance. This was confirmed during a meeting with Ciano at Münchenkirchen in April. Hitler declared that operations in the Mediterranean, the main theater of operations for the Italians, would not begin before the end of the year. The Soviet Union was his top priority. Operation "Barbarossa" was to begin on June 22, one year to the day since France had been forced to sign the surrender terms at Compiègne.

After the May 4 speech Hitler traveled to the Berghof. Six days later, he received the startling news that Rudolph Hess, his deputy, had flown to Scotland. Hitler was at a loss to understand his deputy's actions and was reported to have walked up and down his study at the Berghof, declaring to all in earshot that Hess must be mad. Hess's flight did not overly distract Hitler's preparations for "Barbarossa." In May Ion Antonescu met Hitler in Munich and agreed to supply Romanian troops for the invasion. However, Mussolini remained in ignorance of the plans. When he met Hitler at the Brenner Pass on June 2, there was no explicit mention of the offensive.

Senior officers were summoned to the Reichs Chancellery on June 14. The meeting lasted for seven and a half hours as each of the army, naval, and air force chiefs explained their plans and preparations for "Barbarossa." Hitler made a few changes but generally approved of their conclusions. The following week, he traveled to his headquarters, codenamed *Wolfsschanze* (Wolf's Lair), deep in the forests of East Prussia at Rastenburg. Rastenburg consisted of a number of above-ground buildings, including living quarters, conference rooms, a telephone exchange, wireless station, and cinema, all protected by fences, belts of barbed wire, guards, and anti-aircraft batteries.

The opening stages of Operation "Barbarossa" proved spectacularly successful. By the beginning of July the German forces had penetrated deep into the Soviet Union, capturing 600,000 Red Army troops in great encircling maneuvers. By the 10th Smolensk was under attack; the forces committed to the Blitzkrieg had advanced some 400 miles (640km) in just 18 days. Moscow lay only 200 miles (320km) farther to the east. Estimates that the war against Russia would take between eight to 10 weeks seemed justified. At the end of August, Hitler, accompanied by Mussolini, traveled to the Soviet fortress-city of Brest-Litovsk, headquarters of Field Marshal Günther von Kluge, to view the destruction wrought on the area by the Blitzkrieg. Later in the week, they travel to Uman in the Ukraine, the command center of Field Marshal Gerd von Rundstedt's Army Group South.

However, even at this early stage, there was a divergence of opinions on the major objectives of the campaign. Hitler at first believed the attack should aim to capture the Baltic states and Leningrad in the north and drive deep into the Ukraine, the Soviet Union's center of industry, in the south. Moscow, in the center, was of secondary importance. Senior commanders, including General Walter von Brauchitsch, the army commander-in-chief, favored a major effort against Moscow. Hitler prevaricated throughout August but in September decided to

make the Ukraine the focus of operations. Units were pulled south from the center of the Eastern Front. It was not until October 2 that Army Group Center was able to resume its march on Moscow.

Hitler spoke in Berlin's Sportpalast on October 3 and was able to confirm the extent of the victories won over the preceding months: "Behind our troops, there already lies a territory twice the size of the German Reich when I came to power in 1933. Today I declare, without reservation, that the enemy in the east has been struck down and will never rise again." However, the Russian summer was giving way to a cold, wet fall; roads, dusty in high summer, were turned into muddy quagmires, slowing down the progress of the German invaders.

Hitler confided in his close companions at Rastenburg that the war in the east was over and indicated the nature of his plans for the conquered zone in one of his after-dinner speeches recorded by Martin Bormann, head of Hitler's secretariat, on October 17. "This Russian desert, we shall populate it. We'll take away its character of an Asiatic steppe, we'll Europeanize them. We shan't settle in the Russian towns and we'll let them go to pieces without intervening. There's only one duty: to Germanize this country by the immigration of Germans and to look upon the natives as redskins." Confident of victory, Hitler returned to

*Above:* **Hitler, Keitel, and von Rundstedt during a visit to the Eastern Front, August 1941.**

*Below:* **In the *Wolfsschanze*, October 1941. From the left: Fernando Alfieri, the Italian Ambassador, Count Galazzo Ciano, the Italian foreign minister, Dr. Paul Schmidt, Hitler's interpreter, Hitler, General Alfred Jodl, Hitler's chief of operations.**

Berlin at the end November to meet various European politicians, including representatives from Italy, Spain, Hungary, Romania, and Bulgaria. A Japanese representative was also present. As Italian foreign minister Count Ciano remarked, "Hitler was eager to promote his own victories: the Germans were masters of the house, and they made us all feel it."

However, the beginning of the Russian winter severely undermined German offensive operations. Troops lacked winter clothing and vital fuels froze due to the intense cold. At the end of November, German forces tried to break through the defenses around Moscow; then on December 6 the Red Army launched a massive counter-attack. Hitler forbade his cold, hungry troops to withdraw. Hitler, who had begun to interfere more and more in strictly military matters raged against his generals' failures. On December 19 von Brauchitsch was sacked. Others followed, including von Bock, von Rundstedt, and General Heinz Guderian. Hitler made himself commander-in-chief of the army. The rift between Hitler and his generals had begun. Hitler was also now involved in a world war. On December 7, the Japanese had launched a surprise attack against the U.S. naval base at Pearl Harbor in the Pacific. Germany declared war on the United States on the 11th.

# WAR IN THE EAST

*Above:* A German soldier advances through the ruins of Stalingrad, the graveyard of Field Marshal Friedrich von Paulus's Sixth Army in January 1943.

*Right:* Panzer IV tanks of the 3rd SS Panzer Division Totenkopf advance during the Battle of Kursk in July 5, 1943—which proved to be the largest tank battle of the war. Operation *Zitadelle* (Citadel) was the last great German offensive on the Eastern Front, by the end of which they had lost over 300 tanks.

Wolfsschanze

# 1942

The surprise Russian winter counter-attack at the end of 1941 had thrown the German armed forces back from the gates of Moscow. German losses had been heavy, some 1.2 million casualties. However, Hitler, increasingly based at Rastenburg, appeared far from demoralized by the state of the war on the Eastern Front and planned to renew his offensive against the Soviet Union. In reality, however, he had been shaken by the turn of events. Goebbels noted on a visit to Rastenburg that Hitler had "very much aged" and appeared "so serious and so subdued."

His public display of confidence in the forthcoming campaign was evident in a speech he gave on Heroes' Remembrance Day, March 16, however. He stated: "We feel all at this moment the grandeur of the times in which we live. A world is being forged anew." Certainly the Eastern Front had been stabilized, German troops were still within 65 miles (75km) of Moscow in February, and Hitler's new Minister for Armaments and Munitions, Albert Speer, who had been appointed in February following the death of Dr. Fritz Todt in an air crash, had promised to boost Nazi Germany's armaments' output.

Hitler's faith in Nazi Germany's eventually victory was confirmed during his speech to the members of the Reichstag given in Berlin's Sportpalast on April 26. He made no attempt to disguise the seriousness of the situation that had developed

*Below:* **Hitler makes a speech (probably in Berlin) on January 30, 1942, to mark the beginning of the tenth year of the Third Reich and the anniversary of his becoming Chancellor. Despite the continuing disasters in Russia, Hitler talked in his speech of his "confidence in myself, so that nothing, whatever it may be, can throw me out of the saddle, so that nothing can shake me." Looking on are Field Marshal Wilhelm Keitel, Luftwaffe Field Marshal Erhard Milch, and Reichsführer-SS Heinrich Himmler.**

*Below left:* **Areas of Europe under Nazi control at the end of 1942.**

on the Eastern Front during the previous winter. "Deputies, a world struggle was decided during the winter. We have mastered a destiny which broke another man [the Emperor Napoleon] 130 years ago."

To boost the manpower available for the forthcoming offensive, Hitler demanded that his European allies supply fresh divisions. Romania and Hungary supplied 40 divisions, but Hitler had to convince Mussolini to authorize the transfer of units to the Eastern Front. Hitler met the Italian dictator and Ciano at Salzburg. Their discussions, which took place at the end of April, lasted two days. Although the Berghof was nearby, the talks took place at the opulent Castle Klessheim.

Hitler spent large parts of the Castle Klessheim meetings talking at his increasingly bored guests. As Ciano noted in his diary: "Hitler talks, talks, talks, talks. On the second day, after lunch, when everything had been said, Hitler talked uninterruptedly for an hour and 40 minutes. He omitted absolutely no argument: war and peace, religion and philosophy, art and history. The Germans, poor people, have to endure it every day. General Jodl, after an epic struggle, finally went to sleep on the divan. Keitel was yawning, but succeeded in keeping his head up. He was too close to Hitler to let himself go as he would have liked to."

Although the Allies conducted the first 1,000-bomber raid of their strategic air offensive against Germany on the night of May 30-31, Hitler pushed forward the planning for the summer offensive. The southern sector of the Eastern Front was to be the focus of the campaign; the chief objectives were the oil-fields of the Caucasus and the city of Stalingrad on the Volga River. Hitler established a new headquarters, codenamed *Werwolf* (Werewolf), at Vinnitsa in the Ukraine in July to oversee operations. The initial successes were spectacular: Army Group A, led by Field Marshal Wilhelm List, captured the oilfield at Maikop. Army Group B, commanded by, first, Field Marshal Fedor von Bock and then Field Marshal Maximilian von Weichs, reached the Volga by September and much of Stalingrad was captured by General Friedrich von Paulus's Sixth Army during the same month.

However, Hitler became increasingly concerned at the lack of progress, particularly around Stalingrad, where the Russian defenders under Marshal Vasili Chuikov were fighting back stubbornly. Hitler became furious at his generals' failure to reach the ambitious objectives he had set them. Field Marshal List was sacked on September 9 and Hitler took personal charge of Army Group A for nearly three months, despite the fact that his *Werwolf* headquarters at Vinnitsa was some 700 miles (1,120km) from the fighting. After the dismissal of List, Hitler virtually shunned his generals at Vinnitsa, even refusing to shake hands with General Alfred Jodl, his chief of operations, who had tried to defend List's actions. Henceforth conferences took place in Hitler's personal quarters, among small groups. Hitler rarely ventured outside, and when he did, it was usually at night accompanied by his pet Alsatian.

General Franz Halder, the able chief of the general staff, was the next to feel Hitler's rage. They disagreed strongly over strategy, with Halder believing that the cost of taking Stalingrad would be far too high. On September 24 matters came to a head and Hitler dismissed his chief of staff. Hitler was blunt: "You and I have been suffering from nerves. Half of my nervous exhaustion is due to you. It is not worth it to go on. We need National Socialist ardor now, not professional ability. I cannot expect this of an officer of the old school such as you." Halder was replaced by the more pliable and less experienced General Kurt von Zeitzler.

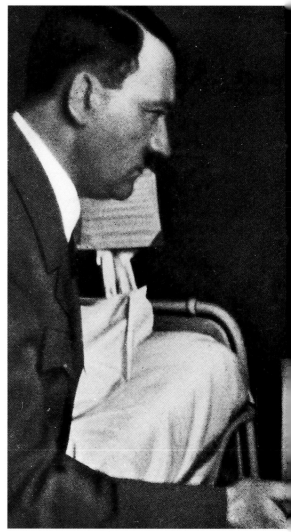

Although the situation in the east deteriorated further during October and November, Hitler traveled to Munich on November 8 to give his usual address on the anniversary of the 1923 Beer Hall Putsch.

He attempted to reassure those present that his will to win a great victory was undiminished: "all our enemies may rest assured that while Germany of that time [World War 1] laid

*Left:* **Hitler and Albert Speer in the** *Wolfsschanze,* **Rastenburg, March 23, 1942. On February 8, 1942, Fritz Todt, Minister for Armaments and Production, offered Albert Speer a lift back from Rastenburg to Berlin. Speer, tired after a long session with Hitler, turned him down. Todt's aircraft crashed on take-off and Speer replaced him. He would perform brilliantly in the role.**

*Below:* **While on a visit to Reinsdorf Hospital Hitler stops to talk to a soldier wounded while fighting on the Russian Front.**

*Below right:* **Young Germans congratulate Hitler during his birthday celebrations at the** *Wolfsschanze,* **1942.**

down its arms at a quarter to 12, I on principle have never finished before five minutes past 12." Many in the crowd could not help notice that the confident, strident tones of the orator of old had gone.

November 1942 was a turning point in World War 2. At the beginning of the month, the British inflicted a major defeat of General Erwin Rommel's forces in North Africa and on the 8th, American and British forces launched Operation "Torch," landing forces along the coast of North Africa, thereby forcing Rommel to fight on two fronts. On November 19, the Red Army launched a massive offensive against the flanks of Army Group B and quickly surrounded von Paulus's Sixth Army at Stalingrad. Hitler forbade any retreat by his forces at Stalingrad and North Africa, effectively condemning them to defeat.

Hitler traveled to Berchtesgaden immediately after the Munich speech, seemingly unconcerned by the recent reversal of fortune. Leading generals, among them Jodl and General Wilhelm Keitel, chief of staff of the armed forces high command,

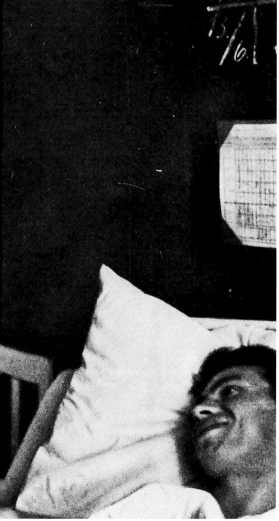

were nearby, but various operations staff languished in a train at Salzburg station, and the general staff was far away, at Angerburg in East Prussia. What was needed was decisive, coordinated action to deal with the various crises. Hitler, however, avoided meetings and laid no plans. He did, however, meet Ciano and Vichy France's Pierre Laval shortly after the Allied landing in North Africa. Laval was told that Vichy France would be occupied by German troops.

Hitler returned to Rastenburg during the evening of November 23 and was finally confronted by his senior staff. Zeitzler argued that the Sixth Army should be allowed to break out of the Stalingrad pocket, Keitel stated that there should be no withdrawal, and Jodl suggested adopting a policy of wait and see. Hitler turned to Zeitzler: "You see, Herr General, I am not alone in my opinion. It is shared by both of these officers, whose rank is higher than yours. I will therefore abide by my previous decisions." Hitler's commitment to continuing the war in the Eastern Front was confirmed during a meeting with Ciano at Rastenburg in December. Ciano, at Mussolini's behest, argued that the Axis forces in the east should withdraw to reduce the length of the front line. Hitler dismissed the argument out of hand. The fate of the defenders of Stalingrad was sealed

*Below:* **Business as usual on Hitler's birthday, April 20, 1942. Discussion of the situation between Hitler, Göring, and Keitel in the** *Wolfsschanze.*

*Right:* **Adolf Hitler in front of a Junkers Ju52 during a visit to the Russian Front.**

*Below right:* **Hitler greeting Subhas Chandra Bose in the** *Wolfsschanze.* **An anti-British Indian nationalist leader who supported the Axis cause, Bose is believed to have died on Formosa (Taiwan) in 1945. On the left is interpreter Dr. Paul Schmidt. The picture was taken by Heinrich Hoffmann, and published June 1, 1942.**

*Left:* **At the map table. From the left: ?, Field Marshal Wilhelm Keitel, Chief of Staff of the Armed Forces High Command, Hitler, and Field Marshal Wilhelm Ritter von Leeb, Commander of Army Group C during the 1940 invasion of France.**

*Below left:* **The early years—Hitler with Werner von Fritsch, the Army's Commander-in-Chief, and General Werner von Blomberg, the Minister of Defense. Both of them were sacked in 1938.**

*Below:* **Hitler with the new Commander-in-Chief of the Army, Generaloberst Walter von Brauchitsch (right), and the commanding general of 2nd Army Corps, General Johannes von Blaskowitz, during exercises at Gross-Born August 20, 1939.**

*Right:* **Hitler making a visit to the Polish front, 1939. From the right: Walter von Reichenau, commander of the 10th Army during the invasion, Paul Schmidt, Hitler's interpreter, Karl Wolff, Himmler's adjutant, Hitler, Himmler, and Erich von Manstein, probably Hitler's greatest general.**

*Below right:* **On the same visit—from the left: Bodenschatz, Wolff, Bormann, Keitel, Hitler, Rommel, Paulus, ? hidden behind von Reichenau.**

*Above left:* Discussion of the situation in Hitler's headquarters, 1939. From the left: Göring, General Karl-Heinrich Bodenschatz, Göring's liaison officer with the armed forces' high command, Keitel, Hitler, von Ribbentrop.

*Left:* Hitler in discussion with von Reichenau during the Polish campaign in 1939. From centre left: Hitler, Bodenschatz, von Reichenau, Rommel.

*Above:* Discussion of the situation—probably in the *Wolfsschanze*—sometime around 1940-41. Attending are, from the right: Keitel, Hitler, von Brauchitsch, and Paulus.

*Right:* German armored expert General Heinz Guderian visits the fighting front. Guderian was dismissed by Hitler on December 25, 1941, following a major Russian counter-attack on the Eastern Front.

# 1943

The opening weeks of 1943 brought little cheer to Hitler, his staff, and the members of the Wehrmacht's high command in the *Wolfsschanze*. The situation at Stalingrad was deteriorating rapidly. In the final days of January, General Friedrich von Paulus, commander of the German Sixth Army trapped at Stalingrad, sent a desperate message to Hitler which stated that he no longer had the means to continue the unequal struggle against the Red Army. Hitler replied tersely: "Capitulation is impossible. The Sixth Army will do its historic duty at Stalingrad until the last man, in order to make possible the reconstruction of the Eastern Front." Von Paulus, promoted to field marshal at the last moment, ignored Hitler's order to fight to the last man and surrendered to the Soviet Union on the 31st.

Stalingrad was a catastrophe. The Germans had lost 22 divisions along with some 60,000 vehicles, 1,500 tanks, and 6,000 guns in the debacle, yet at a meeting at Rastenburg on February 1, Hitler showed little immediate concern for the fate of his soldiers. He expressed amazement at von Paulus's actions: "the man should have shot himself. What hurts me most is that I promoted him to field marshal. That's the last field marshal I shall appoint in this war."

Hitler had by now settled into a daily routine behind the security fences, guard posts, and barbed wire at the *Wolfsschanze*. The key meeting of the day was the midday con-

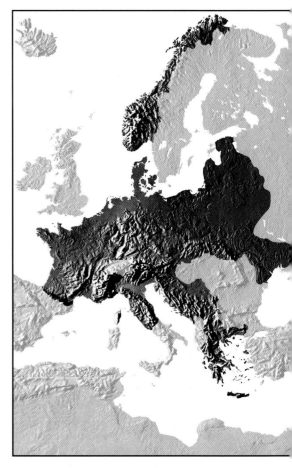

*Below left:* **Germany's boundaries and conquered territories at the end of 1943.**

*Below:* **Remembrance Day 1943—from right to left: Hitler, Dönitz, Göring, Keitel, Himmler, Field Marshal Milch.**

ference. Hitler was attended by a variety of officers but among those almost always present were Generals Wilhelm Keitel and Alfred Jodl, the chiefs of staff of the army, navy, and air force or their deputies, the representatives of the SS and Joachim von Ribbentrop, the foreign minister. Various others ministers and leading Nazis attended on a less regular basis. The meetings began with the various representatives making their reports, to which Hitler responded. There was rarely any discussion of issues. Those present were there to report and then put into action Hitler's orders. Meetings could last anything up to three hours.

Hitler's days at the *Wolfsschanze* were often filled with other meetings. As the war situation deteriorated throughout 1943, there were sometimes military meetings late in the evening, or Hitler would discuss other matters with leading Nazis, including the almost ever-present Martin Bormann, the chief of Hitler's secretariat. Hitler's personal regime began late in the morning. He rose late and then ate his breakfast alone. Eva Braun, his companion, was invariably left at Obersalzberg.

Lunch at the Wolf's Lair, which took place after the midday conference, could begin at any time between two and five o'clock in the afternoon. After Hitler rested, the evening meeting usually began at six o'clock and the evening meal taken

between eight o'clock and midnight. After the late meal, Hitler often gave one of his "table talk" monologues or, increasingly unusual as the war situation worsened, watched movies—mainly westerns. Music, one of Hitler's passions, was rarely listened to after the disaster at Stalingrad. Discussion of the war was expressly forbidden during this time; Hitler preferred to discourse on his views on history, his youth, and the early days of the Nazi Party. Among those who attended these late-night gatherings that often stretched into the early hours were Hitler's personal physician, Dr. Theodor Morell, and his adjutant, Julius Schaub.

Hitler took little exercise at Rastenburg apart from walking the Alsatian, Blondi, given to him by Martin Bormann to cheer him up after the defeat at Stalingrad. Hitler was slowly cutting himself off from the German people—he rarely made appearances in public—and began to distance himself from all but his closest advisers. He even began to dispense with inviting those who had attended the evening meeting to dinner. Increasingly, he would dine alone or with his secretaries. Gloomy and forbidding at the best of times, Rastenburg became even more oppressive as Hitler withdrew into himself and the war turned decisively against Germany.

Hitler still believed that the worsening situation on the Eastern Front could be turned around, although the Soviet Union had capitalized on its victory at Stalingrad by driving farther west. On February 17 Hitler paid a visit to the headquarters of his Army Group South commander, Field Marshal Erich von Manstein, and agreed his plan to recapture the recently lost city of Kharkov. This was accomplished by March 11. On March 13 Hitler traveled to the field headquarters of Field Marshal Günther von Kluge's Army Group Center. The army group's recent withdrawal had shortened the front, thereby allowing for the build-up a strategic reserve that could be used to spearhead a planned summer offensive against the Kursk salient.

On May 31 Hitler attended a meeting in Berlin to discuss the forthcoming offensive against the Kursk salient on the Eastern Front. Several of those present expressed grave doubts that the forces committed to the offensive, Operation *"Zitadelle"*

*Above right:* **From June 25 to July 7 a delegation of Turkish army officers under General-Colonel Cemil Zahit Toydemyr visited German troops and examined their tactics and weaponry. The day before they left they went to Rastenburg and were received by Hitler and Keitel. Toydemyr is on Hitler's left, walking in front of Keitel.**

*Right:* **Discussion in the *Wolfsschanze* on August 10, 1943. Göring, Hitler, and Speer walk in front of Bormann, von Puffremmer, and Otto Günsche, Hitler's SS adjutant.**

(Citadel), would be strong enough to break through the north and southern shoulders of the extensive Soviet defense lines around Kursk. General Heinz Guderian, appointed to the position of Inspector-General of Armored Troops in late February, had a brief personal conversation with Hitler after the meeting and argued that the offensive was too risky. Hitler offered no defense of the plan, simply stating that, "Whenever I think of this attack my stomach turns over." Only General Keitel, who was by Hitler's side, offered a justification for launching Operation "Citadel": "We must attack for political reasons."

Despite Guderian's protestations and those of others, the attack was launched on July 5. Hitler, increasingly disillusioned with the performance of the regular army, gave the honor of leading the offensive to the Waffen SS's armored divisions. These, he believed, could be relied up to fight for the cause of National Socialism.

If the shifting events on the Eastern Front were causing difficulties for Hitler and his staff at Rastenburg, events in North Africa and Italy during the late spring and early summer were equally worrying. Hitler was concerned that Mussolini was loosing his grip on Italy. A meeting was arranged between the two at Salzburg for the middle of April. Mussolini, now little more than a figurehead, arrived looking tired, ill, and dejected, yet Hitler believed he was able to reinvigorate the dictator. Commenting on the outcome of their meetings which took place over four days, Hitler said, somewhat over-optimistically, that Mussolini had arrived "like a broken old man" but "left in fine fettle, eager for action."

However, events in the Mediterranean theater continued to deteriorate. The Axis forces in North Africa surrendered in May and the Allies invaded Sicily in early July. Mussolini wanted to end Italy's alliance with Germany, but when he met with Hitler at Feltre in northern Italy on July 19, Mussolini said little during the three-hour talks. Hitler launched into a long speech in German, arguing that Italy had to continue the war. He stated: "If anyone tells me that our tasks can be left to another generation, I reply that this is not the case. No one can say that the future generation will be a generation of giants. Germany took 30 years to recover [from World War 1]; Rome never rose again. This is the voice of history."

Mussolini returned to Rome but was stripped of his rank and placed under arrest by a group of leading Italian fascists on the evening of the 25th. Hitler, back at Rastenburg, convened a meeting the same night to deal with the worsening situation in Italy. His generals, including Alfred Jodl, the Wehrmacht's chief of operations, urged caution until events became clearer. Hitler argued for immediate action, including arresting the ringleaders of the coup, at first. "Then you'll see," Hitler stated to the gathered staff, "they'll turn limp as a rag, and in two or three days there'll be another overthrow of the government."

Hitler did not move against the new Italian leadership immediately, however, though he began increasing his troops levels in Italy. The public announcement of Italy's armistice with the Allies was made on September 8 and caught him slightly off guard—he was away from Rastenburg visiting the headquarters of Army Group South at Zaporozhe in the Ukraine, where its commander, Field Marshal Erich von Manstein, was struggling to contain the Soviet counter-attacks following the German defeat in the Battle of Kursk. Hitler's crisis meeting with von Manstein was the last time he visited an army headquarters in the field.

Hitler ordered Goebbels to fly to Rastenburg for talks on the developing situation in Italy. Hitler fumed against the armistice in Italy. Goebbels was able to get Hitler's agreement to give a broadcast on the situation. This was made from Rastenburg and put out on September 10, the first broadcast Hitler had made since March. Hitler denounced the treachery of the Italians but tried to reassure the German people: "Tactical necessity may compel us once and again to give up something on some front in this gigantic fateful struggle, but it will never break the ring of steel that protects the Reich."

*Below:* Hitler greets party officials at the *Wolfsschanze*, on October 10, 1943. From the left: Rudolf Jordan Gauleiter of Magdeburg-Anhalt, August Eigrüber Gauleiter of the Upper Danube, Baldur von Schirach Gauleiter of Vienna, Jakob Sprenger Gauleiter of Hesse-Kassel, ?, ?, Himmler, Alfred Rosenberg the Minister for Occupied Eastern Territories, ?, Franz Schwarz (probably) the Nazi Party Treasurer. On the extreme right is Martin Bormann.

*Below:* **Hitler with Léon Degrelle, a Belgian fascist who joined the Walloon Legion to fight on the Eastern Front. One of the three survivors of 850, Degrelle went to Spain and Argentina postwar. Hitler reputedly said of him, "If I had a son, I would want him to be like Degrelle."**

Hitler also ordered that Mussolini should be rescued from imprisonment. A mission was carried out successfully on September 12 by a unit of commandos led by Otto Skorzeny, and Mussolini was flown to Rastenburg. Mussolini was no longer the dynamic leader of old; he bowed with little argument to Hitler's demands during their meetings which were spread over the next three days. Mussolini was put in charge of a German-controlled puppet state in northern Italy, although he had no real power and was guarded by German troops. Hitler, discussing Mussolini's fate with Goebbels at Rastenburg in late September, argued that Mussolini was so emotionally bound to the Italian people that he was incapable of acting as a "true revolutionary and insurrectionist."

Despite gaining a measure of control over the Italian theater, the war in 1943 had turned decisively and irrevocably against Hitler. As the year drew to a close, his generals knew that the Red Army would continue hammering away on the Eastern Front, that the war in Italy would continue, and that the western Allies were planning to open a second front in Western Europe. Hitler, living as a virtual recluse at Rastenburg, in declining health and prone to fits of irrational behavior, was determined to fight on. Many generals now began to wonder if he should remain the head of the Third Reich.

# HITLER'S INNER CIRCLE

*Left:* **Hitler and Goebbels. The charismatic Minister for Propaganda remained loyal to Hitler to the end, was appointed chancellor in Hitler's political will, but committed suicide shortly afterwards.**

*Below left:* **Magda Goebbels, daughter Helga and son Helmuth at the sewing machine in 1937. They and four other Goebbels children took poison in the *Führerbunker* immediately after Hitler's suicide.**

*Below:* **Hitler at the Nuremberg Opera House before a performance of *Die Meistersänger*. In the first row: Adolf Wagner, son of composer Richard Wagner; Mayor Leibel, Hitler, General Ritter von Schöbert, Julius Streicher, editor of the anti-Semitic weekly *Der Stürmer*. Second row: Wilhelm Brückner, adjutant Julius Schaub, and one of Hitler's doctors, Dr. Karl Brandt.**

*Left:* From the left: Wolff, Brückner, Emil Maurice, Hitler's early bodyguard and chauffeur and later head of a Munich handicraft guild, Hess (Hitler's deputy), Julius Weber, Himmler, Hitler, Viktor Lutze, and Julius Schaub.

*Below:* Hitler at the Gross-Born military training area, August 20, 1938. From the left: chauffeur Erich Kempka who as a SS-Sturmbannführer was in the bunker in the last days, Hitler, valet Wilhelm Krause, Captain Rudolf Schmündt, chief adjutant of the armed forces to Hitler, and Fritz Wiedemann, an officer in Hitler's World War 1 regiment (16th Bavarian Infantry Regiment) who went to San Francisco as German Consul General in 1939, returning to Germany in 1944.

*Above left:* **A tank commander salutes Hitler during the Polish campaign. Also in the car are Schaub and Krause.**

*Left:* **Hitler during the Polish campaign. From the left: Hitler, Kempka, Keitel, Schmündt.**

*Above:* **Victory parade after the western campaign, Berlin, 1940. On the balcony of the Reichs Chancellery. From the left: Hitler, Heinrich Hoffmann, Hitler's photographer and the man who introduced him to Eva Braun, Günsche, Göring, and Bodenschatz.**

*Right:* **Eva Braun, mistress for 12 years, wife for one day. She spent most of the war in Berchtesgaden and was kept in the background. On April 15, 1945 she disobeyed Hitler's orders and stayed in the *Führerbunker*: she would join him in suicide on the 30th.**

# 1944

By the beginning of 1944, it was clear that the strategic initiative in the war had swung decisively in favor of the Allies. Hitler was becoming more and more withdrawn from his military commanders and the German people. He was rarely seen in public and spent most of his time at Rastenburg, deep in the forests of East Prussia, although he made trips to Berchtesgaden. If he did speak to the German people, it was not at a public meeting but by radio broadcast.

On January 30, Hitler gave one of his rare public broadcasts from his headquarters. He stated his views on the strategic situation: "There can only be one victor in this war, either Germany or the Soviet Union. Germany's victory means the preservation of Europe; Soviet Russia's means its destruction." To Hitler at Rastenburg, the Eastern Front may have seemed the most threaten part of the Third Reich, but many of his leading generals knew that the Allies were planning to open a second front in Western Europe. Hitler had to be persuaded of the danger. However, from January to May, the Red Army delivered a series of hammer blows that kept Hitler occupied. Leningrad was relieved at the beginning of the year and the Crimea was cleared of German forces by May. Hitler focused his attentions on these events.

The dangerous strategic situation in Western Europe prompted Field Marshal Erwin Rommel, the general in charge of the

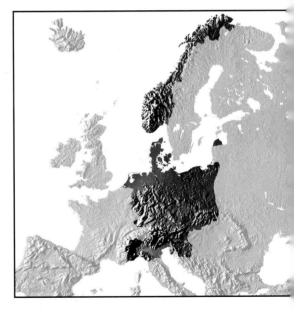

*Above:* **The noose tightens: the boundaries of Nazi-held territory at the end of 1944.**

*Top right:* **A grim-faced Hitler, in one of his few visits outside Rastenburg, inspects Allied bomb damage in Germany 1944.**

*Right:* **Hugo Kraas, commander of the Leibstandarte, receiving Oak Leaves to his Knight's Cross; in the background Otto Günsche, Hitler's SS adjutant.**

Channel defenses, to rush from the endangered front to confront Hitler at Berchtesgaden on June 5. Many of Hitler's senior generals remained convinced that the allied invasion would take place in the Pas de Calais area. Hitler suggested that Normandy was the more likely target, but backed down in the face of his generals' arguments. The following day any lingering doubts as to the Allied invasion plans disappeared—Normandy was the target. The invasion began around dawn, yet Hitler had issued explicit orders that he was not to be disturbed when he went to bed early in the morning of the 6th.

Hitler was finally roused from his bed at Berchtesgaden around midday and then drove to Castle Klessheim, about an hour by car from Berchtesgaden. He had planned to meet a Hungarian politician at the castle but, on arrival, he immediately went into a brief conference with his staff. After receiving the most up-to-date intelligence and studying maps of northern France, Hitler remarked: "So, this is it!" A second meeting followed and Hitler issued his orders to deal with Operation "Overlord" a little time before five o'clock—"The enemy is to be annihilated at the bridgehead by the evening of June 6."

Hitler was convinced that the invasion of Normandy was nothing more than a feint. However, Field Marshals Gerd von Rundstedt and Rommel were able to persuade him at least to

move nearer the invasion front. On June 17, Hitler arrived at *Wolfsschlucht* (Wolf's Glen) II, the headquarters a little way north of Soissons, at Margival, which had been originally created to oversee the abortive invasion of England in the summer of 1940. The meeting was ill-tempered. The assembled generals stood motionless while Hitler raged against their incompetence. The officers present tried to get him to agreed to a withdrawal of troops from the Contentin Peninsula and the redeployment of reserves from the Pas de Calais. Hitler rejected both suggestions. Following a brief meal, he did agree to travel to the army's front-line headquarters in France on the 19th. Hitler, however, never made the visit; he returned to Berchtesgaden. At the end of the month von Rundstedt was sacked and replaced by Field Marshal Günther von Kluge.

Hitler's increasing distrust of his generals intensified during his brief visit to *Wolfsschlucht*. His personal bodyguard had stood guard during the meal with von Rundstedt and Rommel, and he had did not begin eating until his food had been tasted, presumably for poison. Hitler may have suspected their loyalty. Certainly, German officers were plotting his assassination. On June 20 a much-decorated officer, Graf Claus Schenk von Stauffenberg, had been appointed chief-of-staff to General Friedrich Fromm, a position that allowed him access to meetings attended by Hitler. Stauffenberg gained access to the Berghof on several occasion during early July, but his plan to kill Hitler with a bomb failed on each occasion.

In the end the actual assassination attempt did not take place at the Berghof. Shortly before Stauffenberg's last attempt there on July 15, Hitler returned to his headquarters at Rastenburg in East Prussia. As his entourage was preparing to leave the Berghof, Hitler returned to the building, stood before its large window, and remarked to one of those present that he would probably never return to his favorite home. Von Stauffenberg was ordered to report for duty at Rastenburg a few days later, on July 20.

The meeting that von Stauffenberg was to attend took place in one of the Rastenburg compound's buildings, the *Gastebaracke*. Light filtered into this large wooden-clad concrete structure through three windows. The interior was dominated by a large oak map table. The scheduled meeting, due to begin at one o'clock in the afternoon, was brought forward by half an hour as Hitler was due to welcome Mussolini in the early afternoon. Von Stauffenberg arrived at the meeting seven minutes late. He carried a briefcase containing, crucially, the only one of two time-bombs he had had time to arm; he had five minutes to plant the bomb before it exploded. Stauffenberg was able to get within some 12ft (c. 4m) of Hitler and placed the bomb against one of the table's heavy legs. He made his excus-

*Above and Right:* **The general's bomb plot at the *Wolfsschanze* on July 20, 1944, came very close to killing Hitler. Here he is seen shortly after the event (Above) and later in the day showing Mussolini the damage. (In the background is interpreter Dr. Schmidt.)**

es and left. The bomb exploded at 12.42, smashing the interior of the room, blowing out the windows, and removing the *Gastebaracke*'s roof.

The assassination failed in its chief purpose. There were 24 people in the room and just four were severely wounded. Hitler had been protected by the heavy wooden table. As he emerged from the wrecked building, his trousers in tatters and the back of his jacket missing a square of cloth, Hitler discovered that his right elbow was bleeding, his left hand was bruised, and that his eardrums had been ruptured but not seriously. His legs had been struck by several oak splinters. Hitler was able to met Mussolini in the afternoon as planned and took the Italian dictator to the devastated conference room. Hitler remarked: "After my rescue from the peril of death today, I am more than ever convinced that I am destined to carry on our great common cause to a happy conclusion."

Hitler called a meeting of his senior generals at his bunker at Rastenburg for five o'clock. The meeting was acrimonious. Admiral Karl Dönitz laid the blame for the assassination attempt at the feet of the army; Göring vented his anger on Foreign Minister Joachim von Ribbentrop. Hitler remained silent at first and then began a screaming monologue. He intended to hunt down any traitors and execute them, along with their families.

Hitler was true to his word. Von Stauffenberg was captured in Berlin and executed in the courtyard of the War Ministry. Executions of others suspected of treachery continued until April 1945. Around 5,000 people fell victim to Hitler's desire for brutal revenge. At one o'clock on the morning of July 21, Hitler broadcast to the German people from Rastenburg: "It [the assassination] has nothing to do with the German armed forces, and above all the German army. It is a very small coterie of criminal elements. We will settle accounts the way we National Socialists are accustomed to settle them."

The July 20 bomb plot did, however, further undermine Hitler's faith in the commitment of his armed forces to the cause of National Socialism. He became more withdrawn, more suspicious, and surrounded himself with even greater security. As Hitler said to Mussolini as the Italian leader left Rastenburg during the evening of the 20th: "It's my deep conviction that my enemies are the 'vons' who call themselves aristocrats."

Hitler rarely left his concrete bunker at Rastenburg after July 20. He lived in two or three rooms. Their concrete walls were unadorned and the furniture spartan. General Alfred Jodl described the atmosphere as "a mixture of cloister and concentration camp." Hitler's health began to deteriorate over the following months, partly due to the affects of the explosion but also due to his withdrawn, almost subterranean lifestyle. He suffered constant headaches and had a bout of jaundice. In the middle of September, he had a heart attack and then had to have an operation on his vocal cords. Those who saw him on the rare occasions when he ventured into the daylight above ground reported that his limbs trembled and that he had difficulty in maintaining his balance.

Hitler's medical condition did show some improvement in the latter part of 1944 and he planned one last great offensive in Western Europe. The initial planning was conducted in great secrecy at Rastenburg but as the date set for the offensive, Operation *Wacht am Rhein* (Watch on the Rhine), drew closer, Hitler moved his headquarters west to the *Adlershorst* (Eagle's Eyrie) near Bad Nauheim so that he could put the finishing touches to the onslaught against the understrength U.S. forces holding the Ardennes sector of the front.

On December 12, Hitler convened a meeting at *Adlershorst* accompanied by Wilhelm Keitel, chief-of-staff of the high command, and Jodl. Senior officers tasked with launching the offensive attended. Before they were admitted to the conference room, they had their sidearms and briefcases confiscated. Hitler, protected by his SS guard, spoke for two hours, justifying his conduct of the war. The attack, launched on the 16th began well, but stiffening U.S. resistance, Allied air power, and a lack of fuel would bring it to a standstill by early January 1945.

# THE *FUHRERBUNKER*

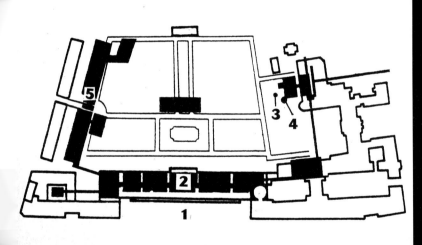

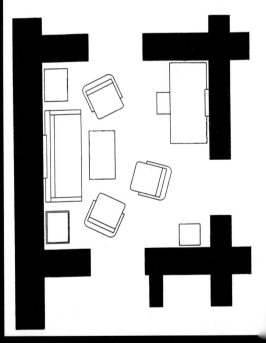

*Top:* Hitler and Eva Braun in a faked photograph produced postwar as "the last picture."

*Above:* The Reichs Chancellery showing the location of the *Führerbunker*. Key: 1 Hitler's Chancellery; 2 Hitler's office; 3 *Führerbunker;* 4 Unfinished concrete tower; 5 Hitler's Mercedes.

*Right:* Positions according to eyewitnesses of sofa and armchairs in Hitler's living room at the time of the suicide on April 30, 1945.

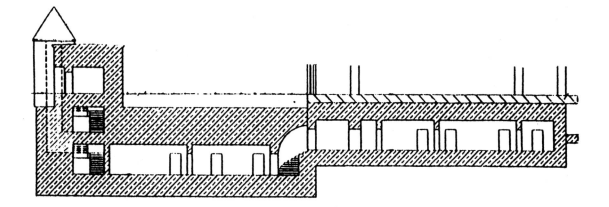

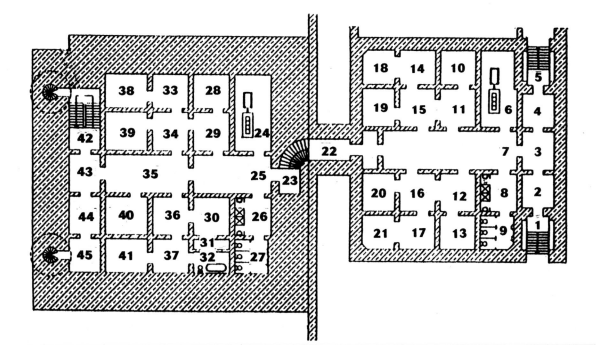

*Above:* Plan and elevation of both air raid shelters (first bunker and *Führerbunker*):

1 Entrance
2-4 Airlocks
5 Emergency exit into the cellar
6 Machine room
7 Canteen
8-9 Toilets and washroom
10-11 Bedrooms
12-13 Kitchen
14-15, 18, 19 Bedrooms (Frau Goebbels and children)
16-17, 20 Auxiliary apartments
21 Baggage room
22 Passage
23 Airlock
24 Machine room
25 Corridor
26-27 Toilets and washroom

28 Telephone and telex
29 Air plotting room
30 Eva Braun's bedroom
31 Clothes closet
32 Bath and toilet
33 Bedroom
34 Day room
35 Waiting room
36 Ante chamber
37 Hitler's living room/office
38 Doctor's room
39 Bedroom (Goebbels)
40 Briefing room
41 Hitler's bedroom
42 Staircase
43 Airlock and guard room
44 Guard's day room
45 Entrance to observation tower

*Far left, top and Left*: **Ruins of the *Führerbunker*.**

*Far left, bottom:* **The unfinished concrete tower see drawings on pages 151-52.**

*Above:* **A scene from inside the chancellery after the fighting had finished.**

# 1945

By the beginning of January 1945, it was clear from the Ardennes battlefront reports Hitler and his Commander-in-Chief West Gerd von Rundstedt were receiving at the forward headquarters at the *Adlershorst* near Bad Nauheim that the great offensive in the west was not going to succeed. Hitler called a conference of his leading advisers on the 8th and was forced, much against his will, to order the withdrawal of the German armor from the attack. Hitler argued that he had inflicted a great defeat on the Allies, but the figures did not bear him out. The U.S. forces who bore the brunt of the onslaught had suffered around 75,000 casualties, which could be replaced, unlike the 120,000 troops, 600 armored vehicles, and 1,500 aircraft the German forces committed to Operation *"Wacht am Rhein"* had lost.

General Heinz Guderian, the army's chief of staff, was ushered into Hitler's presence at the *Adlershorst* on the 9th and patiently explained that the losses in the Ardennes could not be replaced and that the decision to denude the Eastern Front of strategic reserves was mistaken. Hitler exploded at the implied criticism of him and began blaming those around him. Guderian, who had had several meetings with Hitler in the previous months, later described Hitler's physical deterioration over the preceding months: "He walked awkwardly, stooped more than ever, and his gestures were both jerky and slow. He

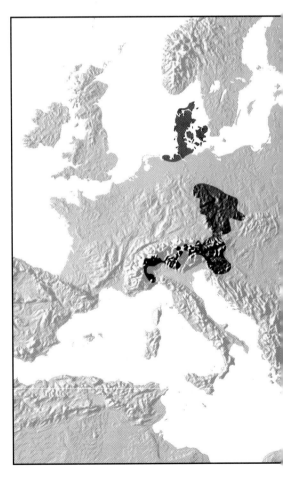

Above: Hitler left the *Wolfsschanze* for the last time on November 20, 1944. Thereafter he would remain in Berlin for most of the time. Here in a rare trip away from the *Führerbunker* he talks to Generaloberst Theodor Busse, commander of IXth Army, opposing the Russians on the Oder Front.

Below left: All that was left of the Third Reich at the time of the surrender, May 1945.

Below: Hitler greeting a member of the Hitler Jugend in Berlin, March, 1945.

had to have a chair pushed beneath him when he wished to sit down."

Hitler's time at the *Adlershorst* was coming to an end. Guderian's view that the German troops on the Eastern Front were stretched dangerously thin was confirmed on January 12, when General Georgi Zhukov unleashed 180 Red Army divisions in an offensive stretching from the Baltic Sea to the Carpathian Mountains. The German defenses collapsed and the Russians were within 100 miles (160km) of Berlin by the end of the month. Hitler left the *Adlershorst* on January 16 and returned to the Reichs Chancellery in Berlin.

Much of Berlin was in ruins due to the Allied strategic bombing offensive, food was short, and power cuts frequent. Ordinary Germans were living fearful lives, often underground in public and home-made shelters. The Chancellery, although bearing some bombing scars, was still relatively intact, but its windows were boarded up or sandbagged and its opulent furnishing had been removed for safety. However, Hitler's wing was relatively undamaged. Its windows were still intact, and the trappings of power—thick carpets and plush leather chairs—were still there. Even the telephones still worked. Until his suicide in late April, Hitler would rarely venture beyond the confines of his Chancellery and, as the bombing grew worse and the Russians closed in, he retreated underground, spending more and more time in the complex of living quarters, secretarial offices, and conference rooms that comprised his last lair—the *Führerbunker*.

The *Führerbunker* was part of a massive two-storey air-raid shelter built some 50ft (15.25m) below the gardens of the Chancellery and covered with a great depth of reinforced concrete. The barely decorated, windowless bunker was a depressing, paranoid place. It consisted of two levels. The upper level was made up of 12 rooms, where some of Hitler's staff worked and his personal kitchen was located. The area also included four rooms that were occupied by Josef Goebbels' wife and his six children, a dining room, and servant's quarters.

The second, lower level, the *Führerbunker* itself, was reached by a spiral staircase and contained 18 rooms positioned off a wide corridor. There were two rooms occupied by Josef Goebbels, and Dr. Stumpfegger, Hitler's personal doctor. The lower level was dominated by a large conference room, which was used for Hitler's regular daily conference, and Hitler's and Eva Braun's personal rooms, of which there were six. Braun had a bedroom/sitting room, a dressing room, and a bathroom. Hitler occupied a bedroom and study/living room. During much of the day Hitler confined himself to his austere study/living room, which contained the bare minimum—a desk, small couch, table, and three armchairs. A portrait of Frederick the Great, eerily lit by the bunker's electric lighting, dominated the scene. Other rooms in the *Führerbunker* included a telephone exchange, a power-generator, guard rooms, and a small map room used for some conferences.

Hitler's physical condition and mental abilities were worsening as he succumbed to the affects of the injuries suffered during the 1944 bomb plot, the increasing number of drugs he was taking, and to the general state of the war. During his daily meetings, his previously immaculate sense of dress and presentation were deteriorating. He was careless with his appearance and, as one staff officer recorded: "His eyes were bloodshot; although all documents intended for him were typed out in letters three times ordinary size, he could read them only with strong glasses. Saliva frequently dripped from the corner of his mouth."

Those living or visiting the bunker with Hitler in residence soon settled into a daily routine. Hitler seems to have taken what sleep he could between eight and eleven o'clock in the morning. He would then have an early morning meal, often of nothing more than large numbers of biscuits and pieces of cake. One of his almost constant companions during the morning meal was his German Alsatian, Blondi, and her recently born litter of puppies. One of the puppies was named Wolf, one of Hitler's own early nicknames. Hitler conducted two meetings a day, one in the mid-afternoon or shortly after noon and a second, which usually got underway after midnight and frequently dragged on until dawn, when he would call on his secretaries to dictate memos and orders. An evening meal was served between nine and ten o'clock at night and Hitler often rounded off the meals with his "table talk," usually a monologue in which he would expound on his world views. Day and night had little meaning in the enclosed, claustrophobic bunker.

Hitler, clearly exhausted, would often sink to his sofa after his meetings. As the news worsened he became increasingly bitter against the German people. Hitler was now convinced that he had been betrayed by those around him. On March 19, he issued orders that were designed to leave what was left of Germany's economic infrastructure in ruins. He demanded that all railroads, transport facilities, dams, factories, and stockpiles of supplies directly in the path of the Allies had to be destroyed. In a meeting with Albert Speer, the Reich Minister for Armaments and Production, on the 19th, Hitler concluded that: "If the war is to be lost, the nation will also perish. This fate is inevitable. There is no need to consider the basis even of a most primitive existence any longer. On the contrary, it is better to destroy even that, and to destroy it ourselves."

On April 2, deep in the bunker, Hitler delivered the last of his table talk speeches. He talked about the political future of the

*Above:* **Hitler and Göring discuss the situation in the last days. Shirer in *The Rise and Fall of the Third Reich* tells how, right at the end, it was astrology and an unshakeable belief in a miracle that kept Hitler going, as he moved colored pins representing fictitious armies around the mapboard.**

world to those present, including Martin Bormann, ambitious head of Hitler's secretariat. He proved remarkably prescient: "There will remain in the world only two great powers capable of confronting each other—the laws of both history and geography will compel these two powers to a trial of strength, either military or in the fields of economics and ideology. The same laws make it inevitable that both powers should become enemies of Europe. And it is equally certain that both these powers will sooner or later find it desirable to seek the support of the sole surviving great nation in Europe, the German people."

On April 20, Hitler's 56th birthday, the leading members of the Nazi hierarchy met together for the last time. Those present included the heads of the armed forces, as well as Bormann, Goebbels, Göring, Himmler, von Ribbentrop, and Speer. Following congratulations on his birthday, the meeting addressed the issue as to whether Hitler should remain in Berlin. Hitler had, in fact, planned to leave the doomed capital on the same day and fly south to set up his headquarters in the so-called "National Redoubt" in the Bavarian Alps around Berchtesgaden. He was urged to follow the plan through but demurred. He agreed to splitting the command of the German armed forces as a precaution against the Allied offensives dividing what was left of the Reich. Admiral Karl Dönitz was given charge of the Northern Command and General Albert Kesselring was nominated to take over the Southern Command, although Hitler, still contemplating a move to the National Redoubt, left the appointment unconfirmed as he considered taking personal command there.

The following day Hitler demanded that the defenders of Berlin launch an offensive against the encircling Red Army. The attack never really got under way and throughout the morning of the 22nd, Hitler order his staff to find out what was going on. Telephone calls to the front line on the outskirts of Berlin failed to elicit any response and the afternoon conference in the bunker saw Hitler rant for three hours against those present. They were accused of treachery, betrayal, and cowardice. Hitler then stated that the end had been reached. He dictated a message to be read out over the radio to the German people. It said that he would remain in Berlin to the ·end. All thoughts of escape to the National Redoubt in the south had been banished.

Hitler seemed calmed by his decision to stay in Berlin. Speer met him for the last time on the 23rd and explained that he had taken deliberate steps to prevent Hitler's explicit orders for the destruction of Germany's remaining economic infrastructure from being carried out. Given Hitler's paranoia about cowardice and betrayal and the summary execution of many of those who had recently been accused of treachery, Hitler's response was surprisingly mild. Speer was allowed to go free. For his part, Hitler communicated to Speer that he intended to shoot himself and then have his orderlies burn his body in the Chancellery grounds.

Many other leading Nazis left Berlin between April 20 and 24, including Göring who flew south to the Obersalzberg. Göring, hearing of Hitler's decision to commit suicide, sent Hitler a note stating that he should take over leadership of the Third Reich. Hitler dismissed Göring from all his posts and ordered his arrest on charges of treason. One of those who witnessed Hitler's response to Göring's message on the 24th was the test pilot Hanna Reitsch. She remembered Hitler's condemnation of the act at a meeting in the *Führerbunker*: "An ultimatum! A crass ultimatum! Now nothing remains. Nothing is spared me. No allegiances are kept, no honor lived up to, no disappointments that I have not had, no betrayals that I have not experienced." Two days later, on the 26th, the Red Army's artillery began to fire directly at the Chancellery. Soviet troops were less than a mile from the bunker.

The night of April 28-29 was decisive. First, Hitler met with Goebbels and Bormann. They discussed the arrest of Himmler, who was attempting to negotiate a peace with the Allies through a Swedish intermediary. Hitler ordered that Himmler, who was in northern Germany, was to be arrested and had his orderly, Hermann Fegelein, who was still in the bunker, taken outside and shot. Next, Hitler had more personal matters to attend to. Between one and three o'clock in the morning of the 29th he married Eva Braun in the map room of the *Führerbunker*. After the ceremony, Hitler and Braun, accompanied by Bormann, Goebbels and his wife, two of Hitler's secretaries, his cook, and personal assistants, returned to their personal suite to drink champagne and talk of old times. Hitler slipped away with his secretary, Frau Junge, and dictated his last will and a political testament.

At four o'clock in the morning Hitler signed his political testament, which was witnessed by Goebbels, Bormann, and two army officers. Then Hitler signed his will, which was countersigned by Goebbels, Bormann, and an air force officer. Hitler then tried to get some rest, while during the day various officers left the bunker with copies of the testament. The 29th also brought worse news for Hitler. Italian dictator Mussolini and his mistress had been captured and killed. Their mutilated bodies had then been taken to Milan and put on public display.

Hitler, having no wish to share Mussolini's fate, went ahead with his preparation for suicide. Blondi, the Alsatian, was shot and Hitler called his staff together early on the morning of April 30 to bid them farewell. As the day progressed, Hitler was presented with the usual military reports and ate lunch at two

*Above:* **Russian soldiers hoist the Soviet Flag over the Reichstag on May 2, 1945.**

*Right:* **At 1.41am, May 7, 1945, in Eisenhower's headquarters at Rheims, General Alfred Jodl signs the unconditional surrender. Fighting would continue, particularly in Czechoslovakia and the Balkans, until the 15th.**

*Overleaf:* **All over in Europe. At Rheims following the signing of the German unconditional surrender: the Supreme Commander, General Dwight D. Eisenhower, with—to his left—Sir Arthur Tedder, Deputy Supreme Commander, and Admiral Sir Harold M. Burrough, Allied Naval Commander-in-Chief.**

o'clock in the afternoon. Hitler's personal driver, Erich Kempke, was ordered to send 200 litres of petrol. The jerrycans were duly delivered under the supervision of Hitler's personal servant, Heinz Linge, to the Chancellery garden. While Linge was going about his task, Hitler again bade farewell to Goebbels, Bormann, and his staff, and then headed for his suite accompanied by Eva Braun. A few minutes of silence followed, then a single shot was heard by those assembled in the *Führerbunker*'s corridor.

Hitler was discovered lying on the small sofa; he had shot himself through the mouth. Eva Braun was slumped to his right; she had taken poison. Both bodies were removed from the room, carried upstairs, and taken out into the Chancellery garden. Hitler and Braun were placed in a shallow trench scraped out of the sandy soil and their bodies were drenched with five jerrycans of petrol. A lighted rag was thrown into the pit, those assembled stood to attention and gave the Nazi salute. Heavy Russian artillery fire quickly forced them back into the bunker. The bodies continued to burn.

Hitler had been ruler of Nazi Germany for 12 years three months. His suicide ensured that he would not see the final surrender of the reich. That was concluded on the morning of May 7. The Third Reich had survived its founder by seven days.